Sunny Skies [illegible] Jay
Jann 8.18.09

HAIL AND DAMNATION

On Weather and Religion

Written and
Illustrated by:
Jann Sayles

HAIL AND DAMNATION

Scripture passages are from *The Living Bible*, unless indicated otherwise.

7501/ISBN 0-89536-950-8

PRINTED IN U.S.A.

This book is dedicated,
with affectionate memory,
to Rev. George L. Betz,
1926-1982.

With special thanks to:
Dick Gance and Gil Gomez,
with whom I've weathered a storm,
. . . and a bright ray of sunshine,
Helen "Gramma" McVay

"I cannot imagine a man
looking at the sky
and denying God . . ."
Abraham Lincoln

TABLE OF CONTENTS

* Indicates poem by Jann Sayles

In God We Trust

Whatever happened to WEATHER AND RELIGION? The well-founded, stable belief that superhuman forces govern the world's weather.

Every so often, a vague reference will "pop up" in honor of the otherwise forgotten combination, "It's hotter than hell," and "Heaven knows when it will rain." Usually, the match is unintentional, a subconscious slip. Sometimes, frequently, in fact, these weather-religion remarks become blasphemous bullets, loaded with anger and aimed at a nearby weathercaster. Being a meteorologist, I often find myself target to such comments. My forecasts have earned me all sorts of accusations from . . . "Damn this weather," "Damn that weather," and "Damn the weatherman!!"

Weather and religion *are* an unlikely pair in today's rush-about world of lunar landings, E.S.P.,

"Outta sight" and LSD,
let's "get down" but let's "get high"

The Beatles sing "Hello, good-bye."
"I'm with you" so "live with me"
"Do your thing," escape, "be free."
Let's all "rock" or go get "stoned."
"Life forever" means "get cloned."

God and weather? Un-foreseen.
It ain't "hip" and it ain't "keen."
Satellites and radar scopes
Mix best with acid, pot and dope. *

Weather and religion? Take another look. The two are linked in a unique, almost mystical way; the interrelation dating back to Genesis.

The polytheistic (more than one god) religions of ancient civilizations utilized an entire legion of gods and goddesses to oversee and modify the weather. Iris, Notus, Apeliotes, Boreas, Helios, and Zephyrus (see page 5) were all members of the divine team that controlled the daily climate changes. The most feared forces of weather, like thunder and lightning, were generally believed to be powers of the supreme diety. For instance, Zeus, the Grecian king of gods, displayed his meteorological machoism by tossing thunderbolts earthward in times of anger.

Unemployment hit hard with the emergence of monotheism (one-god religions). All the climate kings and queens were dethroned. One god assumed sole responsibility for the variety of weather-related tasks previously delegated to many gods. During the transition, though, humankind was never granted any long-term atmospheric control.

Today, meteorologists and climatologists study the weather, analyze statistics, and "project" what will happen. We have no final say-so as to what actually occurs.

We don't do it, no sir-ree.
We work with numbers in base three.
We think, we study, calculate,
Divide, subtract and then equate.
We find square roots of (x + 2)
We postulate the "don'ts" of DEW.
We watch the birds as they go by,
To figure when the snow will fly.
Long distance calls to grandpa go:
(His knee foretells when pressure's low)
With algebra and calculus,
We sweat a lot (and sometimes cuss),
And when we get the end result —
*We shyly state: "It's not MY fault."**

No certainty ever accompanies any weather forecast. An honest promise or guarantee of a weather forecast is impossible to obtain. Computations, visible weather signs, and climatic trends are all somewhat reliable, but never totally dependable.

Billions of dollars and millions of manhours have been spent on research and top-notch equipment, but still the ability to achieve greater accuracy in weather forecasting has made minimal progress despite maximum effort in the past one hundred years.

What is hampering the meteorological progress desired by the masses? Why can't humans alter the weather so those story-book blue skies would ever be constant overhead? Why can't the weathercaster assure us of a dry afternoon for our kid's little league game?

The answers to all these questions are readily understood if the relationship between weather and religion is accepted and not forgotten. With very minor exceptions (which will be discussed in later chapters), humans can do nothing to change the overall "character" of the weather.

The weathercaster on TV
(or on the radio like me)
Can tell you folks about the rain
In forecasts that are very plain:
They're "widely scattered," . . . "possibly,"
A "chance" for some, and "probably."
The radar's on, I feel the heat . . .
So I sit back and rest my feet.
And hope my forecast doesn't bust.
A silent prayer, "IN GOD WE TRUST."

In Asiatic mythology, the female figure known as *Nang Mekhala* was a supreme diety. It was believed that she controlled lightning, thunder, and rain. (See stamp below)

LAOS: Air Postal Stamps
Engraved Perforation = 13
Date of issue: 24 October 1973

90k NANG MEKHALA
150k SUN CHARIOT

THE HORAE
Greek Goddess of the Seasons

GREECE: Air Postal Stamps
Lithographed Perforation = 12½
Date of issue: 15 August 1942

2d BOREAS, 5d NOTUS, 10d APELIOTES, 20d LIPS, 25d ZEPHYRUS, 50d KAIKIAS

Date of issue: 15 September 1943
10d APELIOTES, 25d ZEPHYRUS, 50d KAIKIAS, 100d BOREAS, 200d EURUS, 400d SKIRON

Stamps pictured are part of
PHILATELIC METEOROLOGY
Collection by Jann Sayles

Pious Prognosticators

Bible brothers, men of God,
Knew lots 'bout rain and wind,
They understood that weather bad
struck those of us who sinned.

What is the reference source of the following definitive statements?

1. hydrologic cycle — "vapors rise from the ocean and pour down as rain upon the ground."
2. fair weather cumulus cloud — "a cloud that disperses and vanishes."
3. hurricane — "a heavy eastern gale."
4. sirocco — "scorching desert wind."

Give up?

Each of the descriptions listed above is excerpted from the Bible, a book loaded with an incredible amount

1. Amos 9:6. 2. Job 7:9. 3. Ezekiel 27:26. 4. Isaiah 49:10.

of meteorological know-how contributed mainly by Elijah, Job, David, Solomon, and Jesus.

Elijah earned his meteorological seal of approval by making the statement, "I hear a mighty rainstorm coming." (1 Kings 18:41) Understandably, Elijah's associates hesitated to heed the prophet's "gut-feeling" forecast since the sky was void of all clouds and a severe drought had plagued the area for "many days." But, being a well-disciplined and loyal servant, Elijah's assistant kept his weather-eye open. Finally he sighted a "little cloud about the size of a man's hand rising from the sea." (1 Kings 18:44) This was the sky sign Elijah had awaited, and upon notification of its observance, he immediately sent his servant to warn Ahab (king of Israel) of the approaching violent weather. Then, as biblically recounted in 1 Kings 18:45, "sure enough the sky was soon black with clouds and a heavy windstorm brought a terrific rainstorm."

Was Elijah's forecasting accuracy coincidental?

No.

Is it possible that Elijah actually did HEAR the rainstorm approaching? Yes. It is believed Elijah was familiar with the fact that it gets increasingly noisy before shower activity. As rain draws near, humidity levels rise. This added moisture creates an atmosphere that is more homogenous temperature-wise than normal, thereby allowing accoustical waves to travel uninterrupted, resulting in an increase in the volume of sound. This theory underlies a couple of easy-to-remember rhymes from folklore:

Sound traveling far and wide,
A stormy day will betide.

When the forest murmurs and the mountains roar,
Then close your windows and shut your doors.

And what was the significance of the lone cloud finally being spotted by Elijah's servant? What type of cloud was it? The scriptural description provides three identifying clues that alleviate any guessing as to the cloud genera. The cloud mentioned was a developing cumulus cloud.

First appearing as a "little" cloud, the cumulus cloud often takes the form of a "man's hand," with numerous curves along its upper portion. If the atmosphere is conditionally unstable, the youthful cumulus cloud is capable of rising to great heights, until it anvils-off as a mature cumulonimbus cloud in the troposphere. Oftentimes, the vertical extent of the clouds is so massive it literally blacks out the sun, causing a sudden cooling, followed by characteristic heavy rains, strong winds, damaging hail, and vivid lightning. The cumulonimbus cloud is popularly referred to as the *thunderhead*, and it is because of this weathercast that Elijah merited the nickname "the Prophet of Thunder."

The wisest of wise men, Solomon is definitely the Bible's master of meteorological metaphors. A sampling of his work follows:

> *Disaster strikes like a cyclone and the wicked are whirled away. But the good man has a strong anchor. (Proverbs 10:25)*

> *A faithful employee is as refreshing as a cool day in the hot summertime. (Proverbs 25:13)*

> *One who doesn't give the gift he promised is like a cloud blowing over a desert without dropping any rain. (Proverbs 25:14)*

> *As surely as a wind from the north brings cold, just as surely a retort causes anger! (Proverbs 25:23)*

Honor doesn't go with fools any more than snow with summertime or rain with harvest time. (Proverbs 26:1)

A constant dripping on a rainy day and a cranky woman are much alike. You can no more stop her complaints than you can stop the wind or hold onto anything with oil-slick hands. (Proverbs 27:15-16)

My kind of guy for sure, Solomon successfully coupled his meteorological knowledge with a keen sense of humor. His style has yet to be copied; however, the ever-popular prose and proverbs of *Poor Richard* certainly show signs of paralleling the scriptural sayings of Solomon. (Wouldn't it be a pleasure to view a television meteorologist with similar wit and wisdom today?)

The back-to-back books of Job and Psalms are abundant with weather wordage, denoting a constant awareness of atmospheric conditions in the Old Testament era. Both books imply weather references solely to glorify and magnify our Lord's greatness. However, the two books differ when it comes to how the concepts are presented.

In Psalms, David's meteorological morsels are beautiful poetic descriptions; e.g. "He flashed his fearful arrows of lightning" (18:14); "Showers soften the earth, melting the clods . . ." (65:10); "gentle and fruitful as the springtime rains upon the grass . . ." (72:6).

On the other hand, the author of Job (unknown) alludes to the weather with the expertise of a professional meteorologist. For instance, the following description is a near-to-scientific explanation on the mechanics of the hydrologic cycle: "he draws up the water vapor then distills it into rain which the skies pour down." (Job 36:27-28) This concept was not approved and accepted until *the late* 1600s-1700s when it was restated by Edmund Halley in his studies on general circulation.

Kings, priests, and prophets have thus far been cited as the Bible's most generous contributors of meteorological memorabilia. However, in the pages of the New Testament, it is the son of a carpenter, Jesus, who supplies the most worthwhile assemblage of weather wisdom.

On two different occasions, Jesus recites the significance of weather signs with the fluency of a professor. In each case, he effectively accuses his audience of being more "weatherwise than otherwise," alert to the changes in the weather, but blind to the "signs of the time."

Retorting to a group of skeptical Jewish political-religious leaders, Jesus employed what has become the most popular of all weather-sign sayings:

> *"Red sky tonight means fair weather tomorrow;*
> *Red sky in the morning means foul weather all day."*

The initial accreditation of this "red sky" concept is commonly mis-awarded to European mariners. In truth, variations of the maxim can be traced well before the seafaring sonneters to one of civilization's first weather textbooks, *Prognostica,* authored by the Greek poet Aratus back around 270 B.C.

The accuracy-verification of this ancient aerial omen is, more often than not, right on the nose! Red is a color denoting an excess of either water droplets or dust particles in the atmosphere. At dawn, dust is at a minimum. Therefore, if red is apparent in the morning sky, it usually represents a saturated air mass. Now, since excessive water vapor is one of the forerunners of rainshowers, it follows that rain is imminent if the morning sky is red. In the evening sky, a pale yellow is the color linked with stormy weather.

In Luke 12:54-56 a couple of other telltale weather

signs are acknowledged by Christ: When you see clouds beginning to form in the west, you say, "Here comes a shower." When the south wind blows, you say, "Today will be a scorcher."

These forecasting fragments furnish us with much more than just meteorological messages. They provide an insight into the intelligence and ingenuity of Christ's contemporaries. True, in the "red sky" incident, Jesus was addressing solely society's uppercrust, and, consequently, his follow-up declaration fabricated no flabbergasted faces.

However, the listening audience hearing Christ's Luke-lecture was a crowd of commoners. To them Christ's concluding comment was startling: "You interpret the sky well enough, but you refuse to notice the warnings all around you about the crisis ahead."

The remark gives us the impression that the masses were quite knowledgeable in the cause-effect relationships of the environment. The idea is much in contrast with the preaching of most pigheaded professionals who suggest that all but humankind's elite remained mute and slow-witted until the Renaissance.

Just how did the populace acquire this weather wisdom? Was the ability to interpret the skies inherent to the ancients because it was necessary for survival? Many theories are still being debated. I believe it is feasible to accept the well-founded assumption that seeds of Greek and Roman culture had sprouted in the biblical lands, leading to an accurate awareness of climatic conditions. This thought is substantiated by the fact that all of the portions mentioned in Matthew and Luke are discussed in the early weather works by Aristotle *(Meteorological)*, Theophratus *(Inquiry into Plants and Minor Works on Odors and Weather Signs)*, and/or Aratus *(Prognostica)*. Another clue hinting at the Greek/Roman influence in the Holy Land is found in the seventeenth chapter of Acts. In verse 28, St. Paul makes specific reference to "one of your poets,"Aratus. Aratus was not only a Greek poet but also an author; the author, in fact, of the weather text *Prognostica* from which the red-sky phenomenon was first transcribed.

Obscured in the timeworn annals of antiquity, the absolute origin of weather-lore is unknown. However, thousands of weather-related rhymes, witticisms, and anecdotes are recurrent with the anthropological archives collected from all corners of the world. Regardless of race, religion, or regional roots, cultural collections of weather folklore coincide and collaborate in their efforts to define and decide the mystical whims of nature.

In attempts to become more compatible with their climate conditions, old-timers observed and heeded weather signs. Weather wisdoms were passed down from generation through generation and instilled in the minds of youngsters like we today teach traffic safety. Rhyming verses simplified the learning process, making memorization fun. Somehow, though, the clever cadences were eventually ruled ridiculous and the age-old tradition was discarded.

Nowadays, we have become so dependent on the "electric weathercaster" that few folks are weatherwise enough to make basic forecasts from the natural forecasting signs, listed in Luke. (One of the "wonders" of modern science.)

Red sky, O My! . . .
Morning . . . warning . . . WET.
Old words, some "nerds"
Made them up (I bet).

Guess who? A jew,
Preaching, teaching . . . said:
Sky sign: so fine —
If the evening's red.

Big Ben, Franklin,
Shakespeare too, surprise!
Said some . . . not dumb,
Those two guys are wise.

That's odd, it's God
Thru His only Son —
O dear . . . how clear
Folklore fact and fun. *

I Know How to Spell "Relief" . . .

All children look a lot like Dad
Just look into their eyes.
The weather too, a father has,
Just glance up towards the sky. *

Over the years, a score of intelligent men have plowed through the field of meteorology, making significant scientific contributions. Evangelista Torricelli invented the barometer; Johann Kepler discovered the six-sided shape of the snowflake; and Urbain LeVerrier established the usefulness of synoptic charts. Each of these persons was a weather wizard during his own life span; however, little mention is given them in the brief encyclopedic histories of today's well-circulated weather texts.

Similar impolite inequities are recurrent in this weather profession. For example, the average man-on-the-street goes through life nursing the misconception that either Fahrenheit or Celsius (possibly even both) invented the thermometer. The real genius behind the invention, Galileo Galilei, is seldom recognized for *his* achievement.

The most annoying meteorological injustice, though, concerns the genealogy of weather forecasting. Who is the Father of Weather Forecasting?

Meteorological manuals award this honor to Aristotle, the Greek philosopher of antiquity (384-322 B.C.). His book, *Meteorologica,* written in 330 B.C., fairly described dew, frost, rainbows and other atmospheric phenomena, and was considered *the* authoritative treatise on weather for nearly 2,000 years! In commemoration of Aristotle, the title of weather-science, meteorology, is directly traceable to the original Greek term meteoron, meaning "a thing in the air."

But . . . was Aristotle the Father of Weather Forecasting? Did it all start with him?

No!

Despite his many descriptive explanations, thoughtful theories, and formidable formulas, the Greek Aristotle was long preceded by the *real* father of forecasting: *Our Father,* who art in heaven.

Given no credit in the *Guiness World Book, American Meteorological Glossary,* or *Who's Who in Weather,* the Lord issued the first and longest of long-range forecasts when he pre-warned Noah that there was going to be a life-eradicating flood in 120 years. Dismayed and disgusted by the universality of sin, God spoke to Noah saying: "Look! I am going to cover the earth with a flood and destroy everything — everything in which there is the breath of life."

Not only was this the initial weather forecast and beginning of weather forecasting, it was also the commencement of public skepticism of weather forecasts. Noah, filled with faith, feared this first forecast, built the Ark, and is believed to have gone about preaching repentance to his contemporaries, spreading the news of the imminent flood.

But, no one heeded Noah's weather warning, a trend that's endured for some thousands and thousands of years. Today (despite grossly expensive instruments like radar, satellites, and computers) any type of weather forecast is taken lightly by the highly suspicious public. The long-range forecast (anything over two hours) is an added lark, deemed nothing more than a "dartboard decision."

At best, Noah probably provided cheap entertainment for the motley group of ancients, causing deafening laughter following his most unusual prediction. It had never rained before (see chapter 6), yet Noah, a 500-year-old evangelistic oddball, was preaching doomsday due to flooding. Absurd! No one believed him. Therefore, no one outside of Noah's immediate family was spared.

The rain did come, though, as forecasted. It was then too late for apology, though, with water falling "as torrents" from the skies, covering the earth with water from above, aided by subterranean water eruptions. A disaster of unimaginable proportions.

Issuing the first forecast for the first storm, the Father of Weather Forecasting is God, with his first earthly assistant being Noah. Unfortunately, it is rather doubtful that anyone will ever formally revoke Aristotle's long-claimed weather paternity credentials. However, unintentionally, the weather world has created a "living" tribute in honor of the original divine forecast and first earthly forecaster!

You've heard it, I'm sure, an authoritative, repetitious voice, alerting the masses of impending disaster situations, like a flood. Its name: the NOAA (pronounced no-a) weather radio. Receivable on 162.40 MH and/or 162.550. The acronym NOAA actually stands for National Oceanic and Atmospheric Administration.

This nationwide, special weather-radio network was established following an unexpected surge of deadly, devastating thunderstorms in northern Ohio, July 4, 1969. Pronounced Noah, NOAA is "Noah." The Bible tells us the name "Noah" means "relief," and like Noah, NOAA weather-radio continuously transmits a weather warning to the masses, bringing relief to scores of weather worriers.

If I am concerned over a threatening-looking dark sky, I need not wait nervously for the completion of a radio commercial, or television rerun . . . I simply turn to, and turn on, my NOAA weather-radio.

I know how to spell "relief" . . . N-O-A-A.

Word of advice: What's now projected, ought not be neglected.

Weathercasts of Ages Past

Factual or foolish? Well,
Some have a "snowball's chance in hell,"
Yet when compared with all the rest,
Some others pass the roughest test.

Those clever riddles aren't just rhymes;
They're forecast tools of early times,
When life was simple, fun was free,
More weatherwise were they than we.

'Cuz man could read God's given clues,
(An art that now so few do use).
Instead, we worship maps and scopes,
And plan ahead with highest hopes . . .

Each calculation, so precise:
The weather forecast: "sunny, nice."
But then our picnic's "called" for rain.
Not worth a damn, it's all in vain. *

Consisting of signs, sayings, stories, and suppositions regarding meteorology, Weather Folklore is the actual foundation upon which the remainder of weather forecasting is fabricated. More often than not, weather folklore is of anonymous or unknown authorship, with the date and location of its origin uncertain. In many instances, weather folklore statements are feasible. On the other hand, some weather adages are so cleverly cute that it's difficult to trust their credibility. However, in either case, the trustworthiness of folklore forecasts is in direct competition with the accuracy percentages of high-cost weather services.

Unfortunately, somehow and some way, humankind decided to abandon, if not totally discard, the weather folklore sayings of their kinfolk. Possibly comparable to the creation controversy, science stepped in and showed its sophisticated systems, laws, rules, formulas, and equations. Evolution gained popularity, whereas creationism lost ground and was deemed "old-fashioned." Likewise, folklore forecasting yellowed with age and was easily tossed aside when a more modern-type method was introduced.

Luckily, due to the recent nationwide revival in nostalgia, I sincerely believe weather folklore is on the verge of resurfacing. When it does, there will be many astonished "weather-buffs" out there who had no idea what a precious treasure has long been concealed.

As previously mentioned, most folklore forecasting tips are not recorded with originating dates or authors. It is suspected, though, that many of the weather signs and sayings were "traditional" even before the time of Christ. This supposition is substantiated by numerous traces of weather folklore in the Old Testament.

Elihu, a wordy associate of Job, displayed an astounding amount of meteorological expertise while attempting to justify Job's suffering. In the midst of a lengthy oratory (containing a technical explanation of cloud formation) Elihu makes this choice statement: "even the cattle warn us of the coming storm"* (Job 36:33)

Aha, weather folklore!! Proof of its existence some ten centuries before the birth of Christ, the date chronologists generally agree Job was written.

Elihu does not elaborate on how the cattle warn of a coming storm. Perhaps it was too commonplace to mention. There are numerous sayings, though compiled from other sources), that do relate to the reactions of cattle in advance of storms.

The most noticeable demeanor display of the cow is its tendency to develop a severe case of the "heebie-jeebies" when a storm is nearing. Constant movement, on the part of both a large and small calf, becomes obvious. Scratching becomes persistent as precipitation probabilities increase, and lone cows quickly "make tracks" to rejoin their herd as pressures fall. Both of these reactions are specified in several of the adages on page 29-30.

Also, while I'm on the subject of animal sensitivity to weather changes, a little-known theory exists concerning the animals that boarded Noah's ark. Genesis 7:8-9 states: "They came into the boat in pairs, male and female, just as God commanded Noah." As you peruse this verse, you may not find it too pertinent. I didn't. However, then I read in *The Genesis Flood* that some animal behavior specialists had singled out and picked apart this specific verse because of its significance to animal psychology. The fragment of Scripture does *not* mention any form of resistance from the animals as they boarded the huge boat! Unusual? Yes! Animals normally must be pushed or otherwise be urged to enter a strange enclosed man-made structure. The scriptural passage,

---

*Biblical reference to cattle, not related to the term "holy cow."

though, does not suggest that the animals were lured or drugged by the dart guns of National Geographic personnel. Instead, the biblical excerpt insinuates that the animals filed into the ark *willingly*.

Animal psychologists believe the animals sensed the impending disaster. On the other hand, Noah's contemporary humans did not possess this instinct, and were unconvinced of any danger. Here lies the secret as to why many animals, but no humans, would board the ark.

Continuing our search for early weather folklore, "take a lesson from the ants, you lazy fellow. Learn from their ways and be wise! . . . they labor hard all summer, gathering food for the winter." This is a direct quote from Proverbs 6:6-8, the book written by the wisest of wise men, King Solomon. How ironic it is to have the world's most intelligent man finding value in one of the lowest forms of animal life. Today's scholars, though bookworms, are not quick to observe and gain from the lifestyle of insects.

Solomon again points out (Proverbs 30:24) "There are four things that are small but unusually wise." The number one "thing" on his list is ants: "they aren't strong, but store up food for the winter." The king's statements are made in reference to a particular species, the Harvester Ant, that does indeed store miller seed in autumn, apparently preparing for winter. Unfortunately, this type of ant is not found in the United States (exception: southern Texas), so we cannot readily observe this specific ant ritual. However, other ant actions have been noted that concern atmospheric changes.

Below are several folklore favorites:

Ants that move their eggs and climb,
Rain is coming anytime.

If temperatures are not fifty-four,
You will not find an ant outdoor.

Expect stormy weather when ants travel in lines,
Expect fair weather if ants all scatter.

Ant holes open: clear weather
Ant holes closed: stormy weather.

(Despite all the ant weather information that lorists have compiled, there seems to be no information that links ants to wind speed, and therefore, we must dismiss the assumption that ANTemometers were named in honor of a wind-indicating insect. Also, it was *not* Solomon's commentaries on ants that were responsible for the so-called "Bug-Bible" of 1551. A mistranslation of Psalms 91:5 earned that particular edition its peculiar title: "Thou shalt not be afraid of BUGGES by nighte.")

Another biblical inscription that has weather folklore overtones is: "the voice of the Lord spins and topples the mighty oaks."

Quite early in history, as this scriptural excerpt verifies, humankind recognized the unusual susceptibility of oaks to lightning. Due mainly to their great height and rough, water-retaining bark, the oak *invites* thunderbolts unlike any other plant, and, therefore, we must "beware the oak, it draws the stroke."

The following "preference pattern" was established by the National Shade Tree Conference in 1946, listing in order of lightning strikes: Oak, poplar, elm, willow, pine, walnut, ash, lime, maple, birch and beech.

Many ancient people, of asundry cultures, regarded the oak as sacred because of its frequent lightning assaults. The Druids of Britain revered the oak, believing it was the earthly throne of the thunder god. The Bantu tribe of Indonesia staged ceremonial egg searches beneath oak trees following electrical storms, believing the thunderbird used oaks as a nesting roost.

Looking at the more frivolous facet of folklore, we find that incomparable wonder woman of weather, Mother Nature. It is questionable as to just how long the formal title, Mother Nature, has been in use. However, there is no doubt as to the original written documentation of weather personified as a female.

Look . . . "A constant dripping on a rainy day and a cranky woman are much alike! You can no more stop her complaints than you can stop the wind."

An excerpt from *Male* magazine? *Hustler?* . . . Nope. This chauvinistic-type statement dates back eons, to a time when women couldn't burn their bras since that particular undergarment was not yet invented. This MCP-type remark is a passage extracted from the book of Proverbs (25:15-16). Written some ten centuries *before* Christ, Solomon made this comment.

Solomon was wise and Solomon was wealthy, but Solomon definitely had a problem dealing with women. He was unable to emotionally adjust to the fickle female fancy, and so considered women unpredictable, ever-changing, and annoying (though handy to have around for household chores).

For the sake of remaining a member-in-good-standing in the order of womanhood, I hesitate to admit that we females are unpredictable, ever-changing and annoying. But, I can, as a weathercaster, testify without risk, that these same adjectives are ideal for a capsule description of the weather: unpredictable, ever-changing, and annoying.

So it started with Solomon, and continued through the years, with weather-women sayings fast becoming popular, like "thar *she* blows" and "no rage like a *woman's* fury." In 1941, World War II Navy weatherman, George Stewart, took "one giant step for mankind" and one giant step *on* womankind by beginning the designation of tropical cyclones using women's names, a method officially adopted in 1953. Stewart's idea was introduced in a novel titled *Storm*. To avoid reader confusion, Stewart eliminated the constant use of latitude-longitude coordinates, and simply referred to his storm as "Maria." It is from the Broadway production of *Storm* that we inherited the familiar verse and song, "They Call the Wind Maria."

Once the crime had been committed, Stewart tried to convince the angered female populous that he used the women's names solely for "convenience." Unfortunately, this alibi stood no ground since, prior to the lady-labeling of cyclones, the military phonetic alphabet had been used (Alpha, Baker, Charlie) which was suitable, not sexist.

As society became more understanding of the "certain inalienable" rights of women, it was decided that *both* women's and men's names be used, alternately, in naming the fierce windstorms. Also, in order to cause no racial or ethnic difficulties, names from all cultures are employed. In fact, the whole thing has become quite costly and ceremonial, especially since an unusual "accident" in the late 1970's. The sixth hurricane of the year was designated "Fanny." Personally, I thought the event was hilarious; however, we don't all share the same humor, and to many folks in various countries, the word "fanny" carries a disrespectful connotation relating to a part of the female anatomy. Stranger still, the part in discussion is not the "behind." It's translated to a more topside portion of the female form. Following Fanny's failure, the process of naming hurricanes was turned over to the World Meteorological Organization in Geneva, Switzerland, one of the thirteen special agencies of the United Nations. Now each name is carefully researched before being approved for the official list. Hopefully, no other outrages will occur. It would be a shame to cause an international conflict fighting for Fanny.

If Solomon were only around today!

There is no question as to *what* biblical passage is the

most obvious ancestor to a still existing weather folklore saying: "Red sky tonight means fair weather tomorrow, red sky in the morning means foul weather all day." (Matthew 16:2)

This weather wisdom was spoken by Jesus in response to the demands made by an assemblance of Jewish leaders, who insisted Christ prove his godliness by showing them a "sign from heaven."

Perhaps because of its biblical heritage, over the years this particular verse has been trimmed and tailored to custom-fit the professions of seamen, farmers, shepherds, journeymen, etc., (see page 28-29). The variation, with most widespread popularity, is:

Red sky in the morning, sailors take warning,
Red sky at night, sailors' delight.

It is unfortunate that most reference texts can trace the origin of this maxim no earlier than 1586, usually ascribing authorship to some sonnet-saying sailor. Jesus seldom receives credits for planting the "roots" of this adage, found in Matthew, dated A.D. 60-70. However, it is the very best written example available that defends the theory that weather forecasting was in existence some 2,000 years ago.

The explanation of this age-old adage follows:

Sunlight is white light. White light is a conglomeration of the seven rainbow colors (see page 134). When sunlight passes through different "things," like glass, air, water, dust, etc., each of the white light rainbow counterparts behaves differently.

When red is the most dominant color, sunlight is passing through large amounts of dust, indicating a dry atmosphere. If the more dominant shade is gray, the atmosphere is nearly saturated with moisture.

Since the weather here in the United States travels from west to east, a red, dusty evening foretells of dry conditions for the following day. On the other hand, though, if the sky is red at sunrise, the dusty, dry weather has already passed on to the east.

The spontaneous, "red sky" recitation of our Lord is of infinite value, though, seldom put in proper perspective by either parochial professionals or master-minded meteorologists. First off, Jesus' impromptu weather reference is proof that a reliable form of weather forecasting was in existence some 2,000 years ago. It was a life style — a basic "must-have" knowledge, not necessarily exclusive to scholars and sovereigns. For safety's sake, weather wisdom was a necessity, but pre-recorded weather warnings and alerts were still some 1,500 years in the future. Unmissed, humans learned to read natural signs; sky color, clouds, animals, plants, and insects. All of these were readily available and quite dependable as short-term forecast assists.

The fact that the Son of God spoke the "red-sky" weather words is significant, enhancing the credibility and acceptability of weather folklore immeasurably. Most modern meteorologists disregard the bulging bank of weather wisdom, finding no value in verses authored by "supposed" carefree country cornballs. Regardless of any proven degree of accuracy, folklore sayings are deemed unworthy of recognition due to their lack of scientific and social sophistication. However, in actuality, weather folklore is a compilation of dignified ditties, meritorious maxims and precious proverbs uttered and upheld by some of the world's most righteous and respectable residents. Ben Franklin, William Shakespeare, Francis Bacon and many other memorable men *and* women, including the Lord's Son, have placed reliance on nature's signs and folklore adages to attain information concerning future weather.

Found first in the Bible, weather folklore has a much more holy history than is suspected by many.

We're mighty good at weather past
But not at what's to be.
That's why it's tough to work this job;
(A weatherman, like me).

Computers, radars, satellites
All sorts of costly stuff.
But it don't matter what we spend,
We'll never have enough.

No matter what's invented next,
The weather will be odd,
Ignoring theories made by man,
*'Cuz it's an "act of God."**

Red Sky in the Morning Sayings . . .

A red morn, that ever yet betokened
Wreck to the seamen, tempest to the field
Sorrow to the shepherds, woe unto the birds
Gust and fowl flaws the herdsmen and herds.
(Shakespeare)

Evening red and morning gray
Will speed the traveller on his way
But evening gray and morning red
Will pour down rain upon his head.
(Dunham, *Proverbs*)

The evening red, and the morning gray,
Is the sign of a fair day. (Mills' *Essay on Weather*)

The evening red, the morning gray
Foreshewes a clear and summer's day
(Lewis Evans, *Withals Dictionary*, 1586)

The red evening and gray morning is the desire of the pilgrim.
(Gabriel Meurier, *1590 Tresor des Sentences*)

The evening red the morning gray,
Presage a faire succeeding day.
(Randle Cotgrave, *Dictionary*, *Matin 1611*)

An evening red and morning gray,
Are sure signs of a fair day.
(John Clarke, *Paroemiologia*, 1639)

If the sun in red doth set
The next day surely will not be wet.
If sun doth set in gray
The next will be a rainy day.
(Unknown, *Lines of a Pessimist*, 1919)

If red the sun begins his race,
Expect that rain will fall a pace.
(Job 28:14, *Dawn Robed Red*)

When the morning sun is red,
Ewe and lamb go wet to bed.

A red sunset means angels are making cookies.
(Maryland Folklore Archives)

Cows and the Weather

If the bull leads the cows going to pasture, expect rain.

When cows and sheep huddle by tree and bush . . .
Bad weather is coming wind and slush.

When cows refuse to go to pasture in the morning
It will rain before night.

Watch the heifer's tail
When stretched aloft, 'twill rain or hail.

When a cow tries to scratch her ear,
It means a shower is near.

When a cow bellows three times without stopping,
A storm will come a-hopping.

When cattle stand with their backs to the wind
Rain is coming.

Cattle on the hilltops, fine weather is in store.

If cattle lie down during a rainshower,
The rain will pass within an hour.

The winter will be severe if hair grows thick around the nape of a cow's neck, hooves break off early.

In England, a May storm is called a cow quaker . . . (after the cows have been turned out.)

Calved: icebergs breaking off glaciers are said to be calved.

When cattle low and gaze at sky,
The weather changes, rain's close by.

If a cow thumps her ribs with a tail,
Be prepared for rain or hail.

When water sweats through pitcher and glass,
And cows refuse to eat the grass . . .
Look for rain.

His Name and Vanes

Something old, something new,
Something that we all can view,
Banks and barns and restaurants
Atop their roofs do often flaunt,
Stately vanes of gold and steel,
Indicating mass appeal. *

The first device especially engineered to function as a meteorological instrument was the wind vane. Granted, records indicate rain gauges were in use as early as the fifth century before Christ. However, primitive rain-receiving receptacles were everyday clay bowls and/or cups, accidently found useful after being left outside during a rainstorm.

The first known wind vane has a much more glamorous history. Carefully designed to waver at the slightest hint of a breeze, a bronze arrow was displayed atop the ornamental Tower of Winds in ancient Athens. As the wind backed and veered, the vane pivoted and pointed to the god or goddess which provoked the wind's contrariness.

As knowledge of the wind was gained, the mystical mythological majesties were disregarded. The vane, though, became increasingly more popular, with the information it provided proving beneficial in preparing simple "scientific" forecasts.

The success and widespread acceptance of the newfangled invention prompted many towns and village to display vanes for public use. With its fame on a fast incline, it was necessary to loft the indicator where it could be viewed by the maximum number of people, insuring utmost usefulness. In most burgs and humble hamlets, the site chosen for the vane's resting was the local church, the center of activity.

Gradually, skyline dominance was stolen from the weather vanes by multi-floored factories, decked dwellings, and other cloud-grabbing buildings heralding the Industrial Revolution. As a result, the weather vanes slowly made a silent urban exodus, reappearing outside the city limits on the roofs of barns owned by weatherwise farmers. There they nestled for many centuries, the favored object of many an artist's brush.

A few of the initial generation of wind vanes survived and are still flaunted above their parent churches today. One of the most respected representatives of the early era is the key-shaped vane flying over Westminister Abbey. The stately English shrine was constructed on the site of the Roman Legionary Camp upon which London was founded, hence earning the key-vane recognition as *The Key of London*. However, the politics of the vane have been super-imposed on the religious aspects originally intended for the wind indicator.

Before assuming the title of Westminister Abbey, the church of London was designated St. Peter's Cathedral, in honor of Christ's favored disciple, Simon Peter. Of the Twelve, it was Peter to whom Jesus awarded the "keys of the Kingdom of Heaven," and it is this key of heaven that the vane poised atop Westminister Abbey alludes.

. . . Matthew 16:19: "whatever doors you lock on earth shall be locked in heaven; and whatever doors you open on earth shall be open in heaven!"

Peter is immortalized to an even greater extent by another wind vane design, the rooster. Unfortunately, the origin and meaning of the weather cock are misconstrued by many. It is *not* a memorial to wake-up roosters inside the barns above which they are often flaunted. (This is just a COCK-eyed rumor.) The cock was initially selected by the Church of Rome, and in the middle of the ninth century, a papal enactment decreed a rooster be mounted on the steeples of all the Christian churches. The cock symbolizes divine watchfulness and is a visual reminder of Jesus' prediction that Peter would deny him three times before the cock crowed twice.

Recalling cardinal Scripture verses is also the intent of another familiar weather vane design: the fish. Since the earliest ages of organized religion, the fish has been regarded as the symbol of Christianity. Referring to Matthew 5:10, Jesus selected four men of the fishing trade to "follow him and become disciples," Simon Peter, Andrew, James, and John.

Christ promises the new recruits that, though they'd no longer fish for fish, they'd become fishers of men. Years later, a sketched fish was used as an identity code-sign among persecuted Christians, and even today, the fish remains emblematic of "a soul caught for Christ," seen on Christian jewelry, church bulletins, and altar skirts.

A fish-shaped ornament bedecked the first vane to be made and displayed in the New World (1690). Crafted by the famed Paul Revere, a copper-studded wood vane was mounted above Revere's copper shop in Canton, Massachusetts. It is unknown, though, if Revere was aware of the religious connotations of the fish, or whether it was simply a favored design because of the fish's inate weather wisdom (see below).

Decorative vanes became increasingly more in vogue as the fifteenth century bowed out and allowed the sixteenth century to assume command. An infinite variety of shapes and sizes of vanes emerged, ranging from the classic simple arrow, to the vainest of vanes, the precious Shew Dragon, poised atop a Pagoda in Ragon Burma, with a value of over $100,000.

Of the newer, less-traditional styles, the crucifix and angel surfaced to preserve the theme of religion in a more obvious manner. One angel vane, in fact, earned particular prominence and mention in the *Guiness World Book:* the cherub secured above Berlin Cathedral is the heaviest wind vane in the world, weighing in at 1,540 pounds.

A weather cock that swings to the west,
Proclaims the weather to be the best.
A weather cock that swings to the east,
Proclaims no good for man or beast.

*"There's **news** in the wind."*

Fish . . .

When fish hook well, and when they are hard to haul up, it is a sign of wind.

When trout refuse a bait or fly, there ever is a storm a-nigh.

Near the surface, quick to bite, catch your fish when rain's in sight.

Fish bite the least with wind in the east.

Before it rains, the fish rise, and nimbly catch uncautious flies.

The wind from the south puts bait in its mouth.

Fish swimming near the surface presage a storm.

Cocks . . .

If the cock goes crowing to bed, He'll certainly rise with a watery head.

When cocks crow and then drink, rain and thunder on the brink.

When a cock crows after a shower, clear weather will follow.

When the rooster crows on the ground, the rain will fall down.

When he crows on the fence, the rain will depart hence.

Wind Wisdoms . . .

"No weather is ill, when winds are still."

"The sharper the blast, the sooner it's past."

"When the wind changes against the sun,
Trust it not, for back 'twill run."

"Winds that swing around WITH the sun.
Keep the rainstorms on the run."

"When the wind is in the east,
Good for neither man nor beast."
"When the wind comes out of the east,
'Twill rain in 24 hours, at least."

"Light winds point out to pressure low,
But gales around the same do blow."

"Wind in the visage, makes one sage"

(Howell)

"Do business with men when the wind is in the northwest."

(Shakespeare)

"The winds of the day wrestle and fight,
Longer and stronger than those of the night."

"Wind before rain, fair weather again."

"When the smoke goes west,
Good weather is past.
When the smoke goes east,
Good weather is neist."

Shower Power

It seems to me the question mark
Is Satan's coat-of-arms.
Placing doubt on gospel truth,
Challenging God's charms.

Taking verses that are clear
In God's Holy Book . . .
The Devil hauls in many fish,
With that evil hook.

Tempting, luring; who'll be next?
Keep the faith! Don't bite!
And if, by chance, you do get snagged,
For God's sake, fight, fish, fight!!! *

How many fish do you know? People have been deceived by Beezlebub's bait: shoddy, scientific "evidence" dangling from the end of that wicked hook, the QUESTION MARK.

Do you have fins youself?

Admittedly, I've nibbled at, and felt the tug, of that hook. I was one of the lucky ones, though. I wiggled loose. However, since I've chosen to swim in the sea of science, I'll be tempted a lifetime by artificial aristrocratic attractions.

Being involved with weather folklore much more so than forecasting, I receive the gamut of climatic queries. I've been asked:

Is frost a bit of frozen dew?
What makes the sky a certain hue?
Why is freezing rain called sleet?
Does ice cause chuckholes in the street?

Will raw eggs stand on end in fall?
And what makes thunderclouds so tall?
Are blizzards hurricanes of snow?
What makes the trade winds gust and blow?

Please: Who invented radar scopes?
Is moisture measured with hemp rope?
Will fresh milk curdle before rain?
Can pressure, low, cause me tooth pain?

Can haze and heat make men go mad?
Is Centigrade a passing fad?
Do groundhogs have a fear of cold?
Is there a storm? (My bread's grown mold!)

Yes, all these questions . . . plus much more,
Legend, fact and weather lore,
Each quickly answered (gee, I'm smart).
But then ***this*** *question quizzed my heart:*

Is it ***really*** *possible*
For rain to fall so long?
Aren't Noah and his worldwide flood
Weather-wise all wrong???

What a question! I'd never thought too much about the Flood up until that point. I'd read, re-read, and been read the rather romantic Genesis account and was always awed and enchanted by its hero and happy ending. As a Christian, I believed and never questioned the validity of the story.

Following the inquiry, though, I once again pursued the Noachic Deluge. This time I studied it with a fervor and attitude of worldly wisdom. The laws of atmospheric science, my personal "professional" experience, and my renowned "expertise" were foremost in my mind as I analyzed and criticized those words inspired by God. I copied down key phrases and jotted down questions, questions I had no right to consider questions. Yet, there at each statement's end point, replacing an age-old period, was a new, proud and poignant question mark . . . snared by the Devil's Hook.

Did it rain for forty days? Are you kidding? Weather systems are quite periodic in delivering precipitation two to five days apart, and even stationary frontal systems that tend to "sit down" in one particular location seldom linger longer than a week. Forty days? No.

A rainfall that covered "all the high hills, that are under the heaven"? Bull-hunk. Every meteorologist knows, for fact, that if all the moisture present in the atmosphere were to suddenly "spill out," it would leave only a water covering of two inches on the earth's surface. Enough to cover anthills, not the terrain mentioned in Genesis 7:19.

I thought about this "dilemma"; then several days later, by what some people call "fate" (but I recognize it as divine guidance), I was led to read a random passage from my *Living Bible:*

Stop fooling yourselves. If you count yourself above average in intelligence, as judged by this world's standards, you had better put this all aside and be a fool rather than let it hold you back from the true wisdom from above. For the wisdom of this world is foolishness to God. As it says in the book of Job, God uses man's own brilliance to trap him; he stumbles over his "wisdom" and falls.

Accompanied by a very eerie aura, I prayerfully re-read the first few biblical chapters, including the flood epic. My faith and understanding were renewed, plus, somehow I inherited the irresistible urge to publicly uphold the biblical flood epic as a "meteorological missionary."

The original climate of the earth was unique, quite unlike the climate we are accustomed to in this twentieth century. Drastic differences existed in the antediluvian (pre-flood) days that make it meteorologically unfair to judge their weather with our modern weather "rules" and theories.

On Day Two, Genesis 1:7-8 relates the fact that the Lord separated the earth's waters, resulting in the "vapor above" and "the water below." It's the "water above," this "firmament of heaven," that immediately distinguishes the pre-flood period as being exceptional. A continuous vapor veil surrounding the earth would prevent unequal penetration of solar heat that *now* occurs as a consequence of scattered clouds of varying thickness. Hence, no "hot spots" or polar ice caps existed. There was a relatively constant, "universal" temperature.

We can quite confidently assume that the universal temperature Adam and his descendants experienced was warm. It was a temperate-type environment, virtually protected from the dangerous ultraviolet rays that threaten today's sunbathers.

This assumption is based on the realization of the characteristics of water vapor, the "firmament of the heaven." Water vapor has an uncanny capacity of absorbing and retaining heat. The presence of water vapor in today's atmosphere gives us what is commonly called the "greenhouse effect." Water vapor freely allows incoming radiation from the sun; however, it detains and (to a great extent) prevents outgoing radiation from the earth's surface. The vapor veil blankets the earth to such an extent that even now, with a very minimal vapor shield (0-1½%) it has been computed that the earth's *average* temperature would drop an incredible 35 degrees Centigrade, if that vapor veil disappeared. Alone, this may not seem like an impressive statement; however, scientists estimate a global temperature decline of just 2-3 degrees Centigrade could set off an irreversible ice age!!

On the contrary, a vapor veil of significance (significant enough to deserve biblical mention) would insure world-wide warmth. Presently, the water vapor over the tropical zones is ten times the amount over the polar regions. To a great extent, it is this thicker vapor veil that accounts for tropical havens, year-round comfortable temperatures and thriving vegetation.

The discovery of flora and fauna fossils in regions that are now hopelessly ice-bound is also a valid clue to the climate character of yesteryear. "Misplaced" remains of tropical plant and animal life have been unearthed, in abundance, near both poles as well as the world's most arid deserts.

One of the more significant "finds" in memorable history was made by Admiral Byrd during his Antarctica explorations in 1928. Less than 200 miles from the South Pole, Byrd located palm leaf fossils over ten feet in length. Byrd himself quoted the discovery as "conclusive evidence that the climate of Antarctica was once temperate or even subtropical." (*National Geographic*, October 1935.)

There was no rain in the antediluvian days. This is

specifically pointed out in Genesis 2:5-6; (KJV) "for the Lord God had not caused it to rain upon the earth . . . But there went up a mist from the earth and watered the whole face of the ground."

Granted, it is difficult indeed to imagine what these verses intend us to envision. Could it be the entire world was set up similar to the golf greens at the community country club? — periodically sprayed by an extraordinary, internal sprinkling system.

This idea may seem far-fetched but we do have a prime example of the concept right here in our own country: Yellowstone National Park. Known as the World's Greatest Geyser area, our nation's oldest, largest national park, Yellowstone, harbors 10,000 geysers and hot springs! A relic of civilization past?

Again, rain was a nonentity until flood time. No rain had ever fallen, yet suddenly "the rain came down in mighty torrents from the sky." (Genesis 7:10) This initial rain statement, concerning the flood's commencement, is a concise explication effectively relaying the irreversibility of the condition. It is not mentioned that forewarning drizzle drops, or light rain, preceded the final moment when the "windows of heaven were opened."

The forty-day duration of the perpetual rainfall is significant in that it provides hyetologists and other experts a basis for "guestimating" the thickness of the "firmament of the heaven," the afore-mentioned earth-enveloping vapor veil. Likewise, the veil thickness is the key to the temperature of the primitive world. Consider the comment: the thicker the vapor veil, the warmer the earth's surface temperature. Still working with the concept, let's examine what would happen if someone suddenly triggered the condensation of the vapor veil. Once the "zipper was pulled" and the vapor veil began precipitating, the veil would begin thinning out, allowing the air to cool. Remember, cooler air will not retain the same amount of vapor that warm air can, so the precipitation would continue until the cycle had completely stabilized itself. It is quite possible the "firmament of heaven" disappeared this way, leaving the meager 1½% that is present in today's atmosphere.

As to WHAT it was that became the particulants for all the antediluvian vapor to condense around . . . well, that's another story. Some say a large comet (frozen snowball orbiting the universe) passed too close to the earth. Many interesting books are in circulation concerning this topic.

The elimination of the "firmament of heaven" following the flood initiated the climatic conditions we are much more familiar with today. The seasons began: "springtime, harvest, winter and summer" and temperature deviations were introduced; "cold and heat." (Genesis 8:22) No mention whatsoever of any weather words like wind, clouds, heat, hail, whirlwinds, rainbow, dew, etc., are traceable in the first seven chapters of the Holy Book. However, over 500 references to meteorological phenomena are found in the remainder of the Bible. (See weather-religion concordance pages 207-214.)

How can we be sure there ever was a flood? A flood of universal proportions. A life-eradicating flood that spared only eight members of one righteous family? Is there proof? Records?

The Bible states there was a flood, and so there was. This is enough evidence for me and most Christians; however, as we so sorrowfully know, the world is full of skeptics, irreligionists who, at best, consider the Bible a "classic."

For the benefit of these heathens, we must continue to search for tangible evidence. Therefore, hundreds of skilled archaeologists devote their entire lives to digging up fossils, parchments, and other tangible traces that will serve as prominent proofs of Noah's flood.

The authenticity of a catastrophic deluge is also

visible to the naked eye. Tour the west and view the Heart Mountain Thrust in Wyoming. This thirty by sixty-mile monstrosity is a curious conglomeration of miscellaneous rock strata. In particular, this huge "rock of ages" is quite conspicuous by its unlikely vertical arrangement of varied rock types. The layers of rock near the summit are calculated to be some 250,000,000 years OLDER than the Eocene bed!!! The site is even more miraculous if one is aware of the fact that no frictional-stress marks exist on or near the mini-mountain. Neither is there any source-bed nearby which might have contributed to the *misplaced* rocks.

Many other often overlooked, obvious obesities are randomly scattered around the world. Despite their home continent, each is similar in that it displays the power of a great "force," water power employed by God. Among the four most popular flood theories, three agree that water action caused permanent alterations on the complexion of the earth.

Each raindrop alone, heading earthward, hurries along at a speed of seven-eighteenths miles per hour. At this fast pace, when it collides with the surface, a tiny "pit" is created. Piercing the ground and displacing the topsoil, the colloquial expression for a heavy rain in New England is "it's raining pitchforks and barn shovels."

More severe rain damage occurs when prolonged rains or sudden, short-term "downpours" cause the overflow of river beds. Annually, billions of crop damage results from flooding, as valuable nutrients are washed off farmland and re-deposited elsewhere.

Luckily, no recent disasters have been comparable to the Noachic Deluge; therefore, we cannot begin to comprehend the horror and destruction which occurred. Many descriptions of lesser floods do exist, though, which give us an idea of the catastrophic proportions of the worldwide flood.

The United States' worst flood, Johnstown, May 31,

1889, is relived by these words written by the Reverend G. W. Brown (South Fork United Brethren Church):

> *Onward dashed the flood, roaring like a mighty battle, treetop high, toward the South Fork Village, rolling over and over again rocks that weighed tons and tons, carrying them a mile or more from the spot where they had lain for ages.*

Another account from the same flood states "big boulders and great rafters" were picked up "like so much chaff, and carried down the torrent for miles." In each instance, the same message is relayed to us: items of great tonnage are tossed and torn like toys.

It is the power and ability of flowing, flooding water that can begin to solve the mystery of inverted or intermingled rock layers. Easily swished hundreds of miles from their home quarries, hugh rock fragments tumbled and turned in the terrible torrents of the Noachic Deluge. Scrambled and scattered, to the four corners of the earth, the varied rocks underwent further reorganization when the "mountains rose and valleys sank" at the command of God following the flood. (Psalms 104:8)

Also favorably supporting the universal flood case are numerous grotesque "graveyards" indicating sudden death of plant and animal life. Rapid entombment, allowing no time for disintegration, is revealed in many sedimentary rock fossils. Here in North America, the "petrified fish bed" in Santa Barbara, California, houses more than a billion fish (averaging six-eight inches in length) which died in four square miles of bay bottom. (Ladd, Harry S: "Ecology, Palentologists, and Stratigraphy", *Science*, Vol. 129, January 9, 1959, page 72).

The *Genesis Flood* and *GOD of Creation* are two excellent books just jammed with page after page of archaeological evidences confirming the biblical flood. Unfortunately, one piece of tangible evidence never to be found is "official" records of the Noachic Deluge. "Official" weather records are weather observations transcribed neatly into specified journals by "qualified" appointed personnel. These official weather records rarely date back past the 1870's. For information before that time period, climatologists rely on the journals and diaries of miscellaneous and sometimes anonymous individuals. Over the years, though, these unofficial, secondhand accounts have been organized, transcribed and "hallowed." Histologists treasure the age-old notes and mementos, and seldom doubt their credibility. Our entire climatological history of America, from Columbus to Ben Franklin, is based solely on bits and pieces of such assemblage.

There is no reason we should disbelieve these folksie fragments of old-time weather observations. What reason would Aunt Fanny, Cousin Clem, or Mr. Miscellaneous have to lie or exaggerate?

Likewise, what would prompt Moses to formulate a phony flood fable? Moses was a leader of men. A man of highest morals. A man who received the best possible education in the universities of Egypt. What could Moses profit by recording a fallacy? How foolish for some people to scoff at the biblical flood epic.

The Bible is a book of God-inspired contents. Its reliability as a "record" has been repeatedly proven. Especially since the Dead Sea Scroll discovery in 1947, numerous notables have voiced their opinions on the trustworthiness of biblical accounts. Each archaeological find tends to substantiate the authenticity of the Holy Book as an official record. On the other hand, NO archaeological discovery has ever controverted Biblical references.

So if we continue to relish, revere, and refer to the carelessly collected and recklessly reproduced diaries and journals of the past few centuries, we ought to consult, without question, the validity of the Bible. It has a commendable reputation for the "unusual accuracy of the copyists." And, as stated by Millar Burrows, "It is a mention of wonder that through something like a thousand years, the text underwent so little alteration." (In reference to comparison made between ancient scrolls recovered in the 1940s and modern day Bibles).

If we should satanically choose to disregard the Bible, can we ignore the fact that the "great deluge" episode is recurrent in cultural myths from all portions of the world? Over 5,000 years the flood story has endured, in one form or another, in over 200 different cultural legacies! Each story varies in detail, wth local "flavor" detectable in many. However, four basic issues are agreed. Dr. Arthur C. Custance, author of *Flood Traditions of the World,* lists those four similarities as follows:

1. The cause was a moral one. Man brought the flood on himself either by his disobedience or because of lack of piety and reverence.
2. They speak of one man who is warned of the coming catastrophe and thus saves not only himself but also his family or his friends.
3. The world was depopulated except for these few survivors, from whom the present people of the world were derived.
4. Animals play a part either in conveying the warning, in providing the transportation to safety, or in giving information about the state of things after the flood had subsided.

Fifty-eight American Indian tribes place reliance on a universal flood. In fact, for eons, the Navajos have believed the Grand Canyon was a result of the "Great Flood," and many hydrologists now go along with their primitive assumption. Catastrophic flood action does explain the colossal canyon's development much more credibly than does the theory that the Colorado River, alone, wedged out the goliath gorge.

Irish, Egyptians, Hindus, Indonesians, and Africans are among those who treasure flood epics of global magnitude. In addition, the Hebrew and Greek speaking persons not only have flood epics, but also specific vocabulary words for the universal flood. Greeks call it *kataklusmos* and Hebrews word it *mabbul.* Both languages use other words when referring to any other flood. Since both the Hebrew and Greek vernacular are of ancient root, the word distinction is especially pertinent to etymologists.

Also important and most impressive is a tid-bit of information traceable to mainland China. Chinese tradition claims that all Chinese are descendants of one righteous man who survived a "great flood" long ago. The ancient's name: "NU-WAH"!! Further substantiating the biblical flood account is the "coincidental" appearace of the Chinese written character for "ark." It is a symbol made up of a boat and eight mouths!

It seems highly unlikely that a major tragedy would be misrepresented in so many diverse civilizations. More and more evidence is being discovered and compiled each day.

The impact of the FLOOD on today's way of life, specifically our weather patterns, can NOT be over emphasized. Just as the original sin of Eve insured painful childbirth for women of all ages, so did the willfully committed transgressions of Noah's contemporaries and forefathers guarantee an everlasting struggle with THE WEATHER.

The "bad guys" living long ago,
Refused to change their ways.
And so the heavens opened up,
And rain fell forty days.

The weather up until that point,
Was "hunky-dory," yes!
But sins of man brought on the change
And caused this awful mess.

Thunder, lightning, blizzards, hail,
Twisters, haze and drought,
Would not be ours if men of old
Had feared what Noah taught.

So never say: "What's going on?"
"This weather's for the birds."
There wouldn't be a single storm
If we'd obeyed God's words. *

The Shadow of a Doubt

Little critter in a hole,
All winter you've been stuck.
(Are you the one they had in mind
The day they named "ground chuck"?)

What is it that you really see,
When for your shadow search?
Your legend dates to ages past,
And to the Christian church. *

February 2 is Ground Hog's Day. No doubt about it, everyone knows. In the very first years of grammar school we're taught to recite and respect the story of the rident rodent, and eventually (when adulthood catches up with us), we're unwilling to forfeit the faith we've fostered in that furry forecaster. Therefore, every year, hundreds of thousands of Americans congregate to celebrate Ground Hog's Day, one of the few remaining "living" legends in our country.

Unlike other tall tales in American folklore, Ground Hog's Day is not a homeland invention. On the contrary, Ground Hog's Day is a much-modified European import, with an ancestry dating back to the ancient Christian festival known as Candlemas.

Candlemas commemorates the Purification of the Virgin Mary *and* the Presentation of the Christ Child. In accordance with the Law (Leviticus 12:6, 7), each Jewish mother is obligated to present her infant at the synagogue, and appear for her own postnatal purification, forty days after the baby's birth. Candlemas, therefore, is dependent on Christmas. In the year A.D. 350, when it was "officially" decreed the birth of Christ would be recognized on December 25, Candlemas was assigned the date February 2. (December 25 plus forty equals February 2.)

Literally, Candlemas means "mass of the candles." As related in Luke 2:22-35, it was on Jesus' presentation day that it was divinely revealed to Simeon that Mary's child was the long-awaited Messiah, "the Light to lighten the Gentiles." The candles of Candlemas represent the Light of the World, and during the mass, beeswax tapers are carried by worshipers in a procession inside the sanctuary as the words of Simeon are either sung or spoken.

> *Words of Simeon: "Lord, now lettest thou thy servant depart in peace, according to thy word; For mine eyes have seen thy salvation, Which thou has prepared before the face of all people; A light to lighten the Gentiles, and the glory of thy people Israel."* (Luke 2:29-32, KJV)

As far as written records date back, Candlemas Day has been considered significant weatherwise. Besides falling forty days after Christmas, February 2 is the *exact* mid-point of winter; the "dead of winter." Possibly because of this coincidental seasonal placement, it has earned a reputation for being a primary control day.

Meteorologically speaking, a control day (also called a key day) is a date closely monitored because its weather is believed to be an indication of weather for a particular time period in the future. Numerous *spring* predictions are based on Candlemas Day weather. A sampling of some of the more familiar ones follow:

"If Candlesmas Day be mild and gay,
Go saddle your horses and buy them hay,
If Candlemas Day be stormy and black
It carries the winter away on its back."

"When the wind is in the east on Candlemas Day,
There it will stick till the second of May."

"If Candlemas Day be fine and clear,
We shall have winter half the year."

(More sayings on page 55-57.)

Candlemas Day began its association with animal-life in medieval Europe. For no known reason, it came to be thought that various hibernating mammals would awaken the morning of February 2, for the express purpose of observing the weather. The three most common "climatological critters" were the bear, badger, and hedgehog.

French folklore fanatics relied on Monsieur Bear for their Candlemas climate-cast:

Wandering out from its hibernation-site, if the bear saw its shadow, winter would continue for three to six weeks. However, this forecast was not considered official unless the bear turned in place three times before returning to the coziness of its cave.

In Germany, folks depended on the hedgehog to deliver their Candlemas Day forecast:

> *If the sun was shining, the critter would be overcome with fear at the sight of its own shadow and quickly retreat to the inside of its burrow . . . This reaction denoted six weeks of winter weather.*
>
> *If the sky was cloudy, the hedgehog would not be frightened and, therefore, would linger around outside of its hole for awhile . . . This behavior was translated to mean that warm, spring days were close-at-hand.*

The original "Light of Christ" concept is hidden but definitely traceable in these animal anecdotes. Whether led by the Lord or summoned by Satan, the hedgehog left its homesite, annually, on Candlemas Day. When the animal noticed its dim image cast upon the ground, it sought immediate refuge from the darkness because darkness is symbolic of the Devil. In six weeks, it would again be safe to venture outside because of the arrival of spring. Spring represents "new life" and security through faith in the Light.

The animal/weather myths of Candlemas Day were transferred when Germanic colonists arrived in the New World. The hedgehog (being native only to Europe, Asia and Africa) was nonexistent in this locale, so an alternate animal had to be selected if the tradition was to survive. The groundhog, also known as a woodchuck, rock chuck or marmot, won the appointment and assumed the forecasting duties paralleled by the hedgehog on the other side of the Atlantic.

In the Colonies, religious change prevailed and consequently, the few saints' days or holy days that were salvaged, got remolded and Yankee-ized into mundane mutations of their trans-oceanic ancestors. Such was the case with Candlemas Day. Even though the animal tale remained basically untwisted from original Germanic lore, not-so-pious Pennsylvanians discarded all the religious aspects of the occasion and simply deemed it Ground Hog's Day.

Today, Pennsylvania remains the center of Ground Hog Day razz-a-ma-tazz. With a population of less than 8,000, once a year the small town of Punxsutawney becomes the focus of national attention. Since 1898, the Punxsutawney Ground Hog Club has sponsored a sojourn to Gobbler's Knob (in the Allegheny Foothills) on February 2. On the knoll, observers patiently await the appearance of the reigning club mascot and the performance of its yearly forecast.

Known to meteorologists as the *shadow of a doubt*, every year the public falls for this *shady* type of forecast. Recent attempts to downgrade the groundhog's forecasting ability have been challenged, despised, and rejected. Who can believe the statements published by scientists, sexologists, and zoologists that our weather-wise groundhogs emerge out of their habitats only to relieve themselves and/or seek a mate? Of over two hundred animals mentioned in weather folklore, the groundhog is the *only* one with enough prestige to secure an entire calendar day for its meteorological merry-making. Why should the little creature be discredited?

The meteorological magic of the groundhog, perhaps because of its remote religious ancestry, is often more readily accepted than a costly computer-compiled calculation that's supported by satellites and radar.

WHAT does the groundhog REALLY see in its ground-laiden silhouette each February 2?? . . . "Only the SHADOW knows."

Folklore of February 2

"When it rains on Candlemas Day, the cold is done."

"When on Purification the sun hath shined,
The greater part of winter comes behind."

"If Candlemas Day be fair and bright,
Winter will have another fight.
But if Candlemas Day be clouds and rain,
Winter is gone and will not come again."

"If groundhogs see their shadows on February-two,
Men can take for granted: six more wintry weeks are due."

"If Candlemas day is fair and clear,
Expect two winters in the year."

"On Candlemas Day if the thorns hang a drop,
You are sure of a good pea crop."

"The shepherd would rather see the wolf enter his fold on Candlemas Day than the sun."

"If Candlemas Day be fine and clear,
Corn and fruits will then be dear."

"Just so far as the sun shines in on Candlemas Day,
Just so far will the snow blow in before May."

"Foul weather is no news;
Hail, rain and snow
Are now expected, an
Esteemed no woe;
Nay, 'tis an omen bad,
The yeomen say,
If Phoebus (the Sun) shows his face
The second day." . . . Country Almanac, 1676

"Observe which way the hedgehog builds her nest,

To front the north or south, or east or west;
For if 'tis true what common people say,
The wind will blow the quite contrary way.
If by some secret art the hedgehog knows,
So long before, the way in which the winds will blow,
She has an art which many a person lacks,
That thinks himself fit to make our almanacs."

Poor Robin's Alamanac, 1733

Simmer, Sinner, Summer

Winter is a total drag,
a pain in my rear end.
Shiver, burr, north wind, deep snow,
and Christmas cards to send.

Springtime: all I do is clean,
I'm busy as a beaver.
Stuck inside, I'm sick of it!
The symptoms of spring fever.

Summer, man: I hate to sweat.
(They speak of record highs).
Our picnic at the park went great,
(for all the ants and flies).

Vacations are no piece of cake,
Oil-slicks have scarred the beaches.
My kids are "into" rock and crime.
My in-laws stay like leeches.

My year progresses, all downhill.
Yes, life is sure a bummer.
But just when I'm depressed the most
pow-WOW: It's INDIAN SUMMER!

Oh, glory, rapture, total bliss-
The leaves like crushed Crayolas,
So many shades, but blended well.
So natural, like Granolas.

The warmth without the summer's glue
Is comfortable and grand.
No better time to verify,
The whole world's in HIS hands. *

INDIAN SUMMER: The brief spell of beautiful "no-sweat/no-shiver" weather, tucked between the other lovelies of fall, but favoring the best days of summer past.

Indian summer flirts and flaunts its warmth and beauty. It seduces. It intrigues. It kindly beckons us to rendezvous with nature. It invites us to indulge in the sensual pleasures that are relayed exclusively by autumn. In fall's annual pageant of beauty, the competition is keen, but judgment always pins the blue ribbon on Indian Summer.

Indian Summer is not limited to the United States. However, only in this country is it known as "Indian Summer."

"Why is it called 'Indian Summer'?" Everyone wonders. No one seems to know for sure. Simple reasoning would lead the Indian enthusiast to what seems to be a logical and appropriate answer. The Indians feared the weather, were awed by the weather, loved the weather, hated the weather, believed in thunderbird, invented snowshoes, boogied at raindances, and named great chiefs Flying Cloud. If a fifth season suddenly erupted, it would be named after the most weather-wise, weather worshiping inhabitants of our country: Indian Summer. Unfortunately, this is not the case.

Honor was never intended in the white man's usage of "Indian" in the phrase Indian Summer. Instead, the misplaced, mysterious season is thought to have been tagged Indian Summer, not as a favorable memorial, but as a degrading mock. During the warm and wonderful weather, early settlers were comparing Ma Nature to the Indians in the sense we use the slang expression "Indian giver," in contemporary language. The gracious gift of good weather was just a temporary tease, soon to be withdrawn in trades for the hardships and hunger of winter.

Another explanation of why the word "Indian" in Indian Summer concerns the Indians' ceremonial harvest fires. White men believed the haze and excess air temperature (characteristic of the Indian Summer period) were created by tribal fires: "smoke in the hills." Again, though, no honor was intended. In fact, it was probably sheer luck that the anti-pollution laws were still 150-200 years away from Congressional approval, or pale-faced environmentalists would have sued the Sioux and commanded the Commanches to pay stiff fines for polluting *our* atmosphere.

One other frequently heard explanation of the etymology of Indian Summer: during the unexpected warm weather, the Indians would return to the forests and fields and resume their summer labors as if the season had never changed. In anticipation of the energy crisis, white men lazy-loafed inside their log cabins.

Numerous other theories exist on the evolution of the wording, Indian Summer. Some tend to be reasonable; most tend to be ridiculous. Some can be traced as far back as 1778; others are rather recent. (Probably the most recent, and most far-fetched, is my buddy's idea: the Cleveland Indians spend April through August "practicing" baseball as if it were spring training. Not until

September do they begin winning and professionally playing the "summer" sport, hence, "Indian" Summer.)

Anyway, the sorry point of the whole matter is that neither written records nor hearsay evidence associate Indian Summer with the Indians' intimate relationship with the weather; neither do American tales associate Indian Summer with its European counterparts: St. Luke's Little Summer and St. Martin's Summer.

On the spiritual calendar, the Feast of Saint Luke is celebrated on the eighteenth day of October. More often than seems possibly coincidental, a spell of fine summery weather occurs in mid-October, near the saint's feast day. Therefore, the weather pattern is reverently referred to as St. Luke's Little Summer.

The divine explanation on "why" there's a St. Luke's Little Summer follows:

Luke, the author of the Gospel according to Luke *and* the Acts of the Apostles, is also the patron saint of doctors and artists. St. Luke's Little Summer is believed to be the blessed remedy prepared and administered by God on behalf of Luke, the biblical "beloved physician" (Colossians 4:14 KJV) — a carefully contrived climatic concoction consisting of pre-measured, "tolerable" amounts of both fall's beauty and summer's glamour. A dosage dispensed at a critical time, St. Luke's Little Summer soothes those suffering from the stresses of summer-past, and the worries of the winter-future.

And what about the fall foliage? It, too, is explainable as a gift of God in remembrance of St. Luke. As previously mentioned, St. Luke was not only an author and doctor, but also a painter. Luke's most significant work is the only "from life" portrait of the Virgin Mary. Known as the *Black Madonna of Poland,* it's weathered and worn but still displayed in Czestochowa, Poland. For those unable to view the priceless picture, God annually allows us a glimpse of Luke's artistic creativity in the splendor of multi-colored fall leaves.

When the calendar page is turned, the legend changes. In November, Indian Summer-type weather is piously proclaimed St. Martin's Summer. The story goes as follows:

On a cold November's day, many hundreds of years ago, a saintly man named Martin tore his cloak into two pieces in order to give half of it to an unknown beggar shivering along the roadside. Recognizing the extraordinary act of kindness, God immediately sent forth a few days of warm weather to keep the good man comfortable until he could purchase a new garment. Annually, this unseasonably warm period of weather miraculously re-occurs, amidst a month normally cold and suggestive of winter. The pleasant weather usually occurs right around the eleventh of November, the Feast Day of St. Martin.

The weather of St. Martin was also believed to be indicative of coming winter weather. "If St. Martin's Day is cold, the winter will not be long lasting."

In the Fourth Century, Martin was the Bishop of Tours (province of France). Today he is the patron saint of tavern keepers, beggars, winegrowers, and drunkards.

Someway, somehow, somewhere, our foolish forefathers forfeited these faith-fixed legends. Here in the United States, starting from scratch, Indian Summer emerged, lacking all religious flavor and all but a pinch of good taste. Indian Summer (with no disrespect intended for the Indians) is an unrefined, bland Yankee extraction of a savory European dessert *flambe*.

Stripped of all its dignity and reverence, like Groundhog's Day, Indian Summer receives a tremendous amount of publicity. In particular, thousands and millions of Indian Summer questions are asked of innocent weathercasters.

This is it, that is it
No, it's not, you're full of it.

That was it one week ago
No, you're wrong, it didn't snow.
Now it's here. Oh, no it's not
It's way too cold and not so hot. *

Professional meteorologists, in an attempt to maintain some sort of discipline, have recently established a set of strict technical rules and qualifications that autumn weather is required to fulfill before it can be awarded the highest honor, the title Indian Summer:

1. *The temperature must officially fall below 32 degrees Fahrenheit, thereby insuring a "killer" frost and ending the growing season.*
2. *Temperatures must remain below normal for an extended period of time before recovering to above normal.*
3. *Indian Summer cannot occur before the autumnal equinox.*

Waiting for one of these orthodox Indian Summers can be quite frustrating. Farmers get especially miffed, aware of the fact that the official temperatures mentioned in the requirements are taken from inside cutsie little government-regulated instrument shelters which must be located exactly five feet above the ground, due to overnight heat radiation. Therefore, unless your green thumb enables you to grow crops five feet ABOVE the ground (in lieu of the customary *in* and *out* of the ground), the growing season will end for your crops long before the official frost.

So, scientific sophistication and ritzy restrictions have further added to the public confusion and controversy. (Next time there's a lull in the action at a family reunion, tell Grandpa the Indian Summers he remembers really "weren't.")

The religion-based legends remain free of such space-age revisions.

In conclusion, for those of you who are pragmatic, rather than pro-Indian, but prefer to profess no piety, the list below gives you a selection of established alternate names to call the same type of climatic occurrence:

Second Summer	After Heat
Fall-Summer	Counterfeit Summer
Old Wive's Summer	

Regardless, though, of what you call it, whose rules you obey or what religion you follow, St. Luke's and St. Martin's/Indian Summer are the weather conditions that believers and non-believers all agree are: HEAVENLY, and HOW.

Braves and warriors, chiefs of tribes,
Think us white-man get bad vibes . . .
Cowboys with their pants of leather,
Nasty: call it INJUN weather
Let's pass peace pipe, postpone pranks . . .
Beat drum, sing song, send God thanks. *

Saint Soggy

Bumbershoots and rubberboots and
Pant legs rolled up high . . .
Why is it that it's wet for sure
Each 15th of July?

The sewers clog, the mud gets thick
(Despite "no chance" of rain),
The reoccurring mystery
Cannot be classed mundane.

It surely is a rarity.
Coincidence it ain't.
The answer is it rains each year
Thanks to our Soggy Saint. *

Saint Soggy, more properly addressed as Saint Swithin, was priest to King Egbert in the ninth century, and is noted Bishop of Winchester who devised and originated the tithe system in England.

Today, St. Swithin is best remembered in weather maxims, the most popular of which is, "If it rains on St. Swithin's Day, it will rain for forty days to come."

The meteorological accuracy of this particular adage has been repeatedly discredited and often used as prime example to cast shame on all weather-saint sayings. However, the legendary link between Swithin and wet weather is obviously well-founded.

Known for his extraordinary humility and kindness, St. Swithin sacrificed a lifetime preaching to and protecting the poor, teaching them love and recognition of God's unboughten gifts, with a special reverence for rain. Living among the less fortunate, Swithin decided his bodily remains would also be more comfortable buried amongst the commoners in the churchyard of the cathedral. Catering to his wishes, Swithin was buried "where dew and rain would fall," and there he rested for one hundred years. Reviewing his divine greatness, though, a century later Swithin was promoted to sainthood, and the priests felt it ethical to enshrine Swithin's remains inside Winchester Cathedral, a place of high honor. Their work started July 15, but ended abruptly due to a heavy downpour of forty-day endurance. Because of the incredible wet period, priests were convinced their transfer attempt was interrupted by divine forces, and believed the yearly anniversary date of the incident would bring recurrent conditions, compliments of the displaced saint.

Other countries with similar Swithin sayings include France (June 8, St. Medada Day), Belgium (July 27, St. Godelieve Day) and Russia (July 10, St. Samson Day). In each kingdom, rain on the saint's feast day portends of forty consecutive wet days, as is expected following a showery Swithin day. However, unlike the heart-touching saga rooted beneath the Swithin precipitation prognosis, there seems to be no logical reason why these saints are associated with lengthy rainfall. Even so, folklore harbors the traditional forecasts, and every so often, one of the sayings slips into an unexpected media, such as the following article lost in the pages of *The Plain Dealer* (Cleveland), July 11, 1980, entitled "Wet Omen for the Olympics":

> *Moscow (AP) — Soviet scientists have predicted "close to ideal" weather for the summer Olympic Games July 19 through August 3, but according to old Russian folklore, Moscow could be in for 40 days of rain. According to the Russian Orthodox Church calendar, yesterday was St. Samson's Day. And folk tradition has it that if it rains on St. Samson's Day, you had better pack an umbrella for the next 40 days. It rained yesterday.*

Below are the Saint Swithin's Day (July 15) observations compiled by an anonymous Englishman for a 20-year period.

Year	**Weather July 15**	**Rain in Next 40 Days**
1841	rain	23 rain days
1842	dry	12 rain days
1843		22 rain days
1844		20 rain days
1845	rain	26 rain days
1846		21 rain days
1847		17 rain days
1848		31 rain days
1849		20 rain days
1850	rain	17 rain days
1851	rain	13 rain days
1852		19 rain days
1853	rain	18 rain days
1854	rain	16 rain days
1855		18 rain days

1856	rain	14 rain days
1857		14 rain days
1858		14 rain days
1859		13 rain days
1860		29 rain days

SUMMARY: The record check revealed it rained on St. Swithin's Day only six times in 20 years, with the greatest number of rain days following a DRY July 15.

A similar examination calculated that a wet St. Swithin's Day is preceded by only seventeen wet days, in lieu of forty. (Survey period 1841-1904)

Swithin's Day Sayings

St. Swithin's Day, if thou dost rain,
For 40 days it will remain.
St. Swithin's Day, if thou be fair,
For 40 days 'twill rain nae mair.

St. Swithin is Christening the Apples.

. . . commentary on Swithin's Day, as appeared in
Poor Robin's Almanac, 1697.

In this month is St. Swithin's Day
On which, if that it rain, they say
Full forty days after it will,
Or more or less, some rain distill.
This Swithin was a saint, I trow,
And Winchester bishop also.
Who in his time did many a feat,
As popish legends do repeat:
A woman having broken her eggs,
By stumbling at another's legs
For which she made a woeful cry.
St. Swithin chanced for to come by,
Who made them all as sound or more

Than ever that they were before.
But whether this were so or no,
'Tis more than you or I do know,
Better it is to rise betime,
And to make hay while sun doth shine,
Than to believe in tales and lies,
Which idle monks and friars devise.

Freezer Teaser

Climatological colloquialisms concerning canines are quite common:

We have "sun DOGS" and "sea DOGS"
(Both rainbows, you know)
"Fog DOGS" and "hot DOGS"
(With mustard-to-go)

The "DOG days" we FLEA from,
(It's always BONE dry)
When Sirius, DOG star,
Appears in the sky.

The moisture is falling,
It's flooding the ground,
The wind moans and howls like,
A hungry 'ole HOUND.

In that case, we must say,

It stormed DOGgone hard,
Or "cats and DOGS" raining,
*A wet Saint Bernard.**

St. Bernard is a large, reddish-brown and white dog whose ancestors were owned and trained by monks of the hospice of the Great St. Bernard Pass, in the Swiss Alps. Named after Bernard of Montjoux, the patron saint of mountaineers, St. Bernard dogs are disciplined to search for and rescue distressed snow travelers, an act the saint, Bernard, was known for.

Yes, dogs have managed to be memorialized in the weather-wordage used by professional meteorologists, with a half-dozen dictionary-type entries properly listed in the AMS glossary.

Also, though unfound in meteorological texts, certain dog-sayings are spoken with an uncanny consistency when referring to weathercasters.

They're always in "the dog house"
(Those silly weather guys)
Their business is "goin' to the dogs"
(Their forecasts are just like lies)

. . . but, despite all this pet-prose and phraseology, few forecasters are familiar with the term DOGwood winter.

Like Groundhog Day and Indian Summer, Dogwood Winter is an unsuspecting secular title, tagged onto a particular set of holy days by early "do-your-own-thing" American settlers.

Following a long, honorable life in the "Old Country," Dogwood Winter was one of the few weather-religious occasions selected for the ocean cruise across to the New World. Unfortunately, unlike its two shipmates, Dogwood Winter was unable to maintain a high rapport among the colonists, once it became landbound. Eventually, Dogwood Winter became hazed and obscured. Today, only a handful of contemporaries have heard of the once well-known term.

The seasonal reciprocal of Indian Summer, Dogwood Winter is wicked, wintery weather, misplaced amidst May's maturing spring. Slaying seedling sprouts and butchering blossoming buds, it's easy to understand why Dogwood Winter failed to achieve high ratings on the popularity polls of pioneers, ultimately becoming a classic example of Barbra Streisand's song-lyrics: "What's too painful to remember, we simply choose to forget."

According to climatological statistics, though, Dogwood Winter is not easily forgotten. True, the name and legend are past recollection but official records verify its existence. Forty-seven out of fifty years (a whopping 94%) Dogwood Winter reliably occurs between May 8th and May 15th, characterized by sub-normal temperatures, frost, sleet, and/or snow.

In Europe, this abrupt interruption most often transpires May 11, 12, and 13, the days honoring saints Mamertius, Pancras, and Servatius. Because of the annual arrival of abhorred wintry conditions on the feast days of these three men of God, they became known as the Ice Saints.

Unlike our United States residents, Europeans were not so nonchalant about the effects of the Ice Saints. On the contrary, vengeance was sought against the three chilly saints. In France, history reports perturbed peasants flogged statues and defaced pictures of the men, demonstrating disapproval of the Freezer Teaser yearly delivered by the Frost Saints.

It is not definitely known why these particular saints are associated with cold weather; however, reasonable assumptions can be made after checking the backgrounds of the three saints involved.

MAMERTIUS: May 11 is the day ascribed to remembering Mamertius, the fifth century bishop of Vienne. The adoption of the Minor Litanies was initiated by Mamertius, the saint who preached the necessity of asking divine protection from harm, following a series of terrifying floods and earthquakes.

Does Saint Mamertius bring cold weather because we neglect to praise the Lord for spring's warmth and fail to petition his guard against winter's return?

PANCRAS: An orphan, converted early in life to Christianity, Pancras is one of the youngest saints, martyred at the unlucky age of thirteen. In his short life span, Pancras earned notoriety for tormenting those who swore. The feast day of Pancras is May 12.

Does the cold snap early in spring symbolize the shortened life of the youthful Pancras? Are we annually plagued with bad weather due to our continued, determined use of foul language?

SERVATIUS: The third member of the Ice Saints is honored on May 13. Servatius, a fourth century bishop of Tongues, correctly prophesied the invasion of Gaul by the Huns, and is best remembered for the pilgrimage he organized to fast and pray for protection on the mission. Not a victim of martyrdom, Servatius died suddenly of a mysterious "fever" on May 13.

It could be our failure to praise the Lord that prompts the return of winter once spring is underway. It is also reasonably possible that the term "spring fever" finds its origin in the illness that caused Servatius' death. In any instance, today he is best remembered in weather folklore through the adage:

"He who shears his sheep before St. Servatius,
Loves his wool more than his sheep."
(Unknown)

Attempting to strip the time period of its theological significance, Americans immediately reassigned the name Dogwood Winter to the span of days our European forefathers called the Days of the Ice Saints.

The alteration was logical, but definitely not complete. The yearly, yucky cold spell seemed to coincide with the annual blossoming state of the dogwood tree, hence the name Dogwood Winter. However, through legend, the dogwood blossom is a religious symbol of the Crucifixion.

During the era of and before Christ's crucifixion, the dogwood tree grew strong, straight and tall. Because of its agreeable characteristics, it was chosen as the timber for Christ's cross. Acknowledging the tree's regret over its involuntary participation in Christ's torture, God never again allowed it to mature in a manner that it might be misused for such malevolence.

In divine remembrance of this agreement, the dogwood blossoms are specially fashioned and decorated:

> Two short petals and two long petals, each stained with a speck of brown "rust" and red "blood," symbolic of nail prints.
>
> In the center of the blossom lies a miniature facsimile of Christ's thorny crown.

Temperatures rising; alas it's spring!
(Lovers love and songbirds sing)
The weather's fine, it does entice . . .
Until in walk three saints of Ice.

Then, "see ya later, alligator"
It's back to the refrigerator,
Mucky, nasty, slushy sleet,
Replace the sun and warming heat.

Just like a comma in a sentence, —
'Cause we forgot to ask repentance
Forgot to praise God for spring beauty,
That's WHY our weather seems so moody.

Habits, Rabbits / Causes and Clauses

Don't listen to your weatherman,
When Christmas Eve is nigh,
Though he may show you charts and graphs
And tell you what is why.

It doesn't matter what you see,
Those radarscopes deceive,
Just leave to faith the weather and
You'll get what you believe.

It snows, of course, so Santa's sleigh,
Will silent land on roofs,
And wind must blow just harsh enough
To erase tracks of hoofs.

There must be fog at take-off time,
So Rudolph's nose can glow.
But all is calm and all is bright,
By Santa's last ho-ho.

A complicated forecast? Yes.
One science claims unreal.
But, every year at Christmastime,
God's magic is revealed. *

Finding yourself scheduled to work on Christmas Eve in a weather office is a surprise not unlike discovering you've just set foot on a wad of freshly chewed bubble gum. Mixed emotions (leaning towards contempt) suddenly cause a rash of red to flare across your face, and your memory becomes a blur of unpleasant experiences.

The very success or failure of a meteorologist is at stake on Christmas Eve. Predict snow, and instant popularity is to be received, accompanied by unexpected presents and heartfelt expressions of gratitude. But, mention any other form of precipitation (especially those types associated with warmth), and you're certain to soon find yourself wishing you'd chosen a more rewarding career, like sword swallower or coal bed walker.

With this in mind, every year I feel sickness and/or severe sentimentality succumbing me and go to great extremes to be noticeably disabled in hopes my boss will offer to replace me on Christmas Eve. Usually, though, my symptoms are unconvincing and I'm stuck preparing public predictions. In pursuit of happiness, I thereby prefer to relate forecasts found in folklore. The old sayings are based on what Christmas is: magic, God's magic, that began with the birth of Christ, a baby born of a virgin.

Old-timers will tell you that it's useless to try and predict Christmas weather. It is totally special. Like the Star of Bethlehem, the weather on Christmas is a divine sign. Proper interpretation of the sign results in a lengthy, long-range forecast which includes insights on all of the following:

a) The severity of the coming winter:
If ice will bear a man at Christmas, it will not bear a mouse afterward.

The nearer to a new moon on Christmas, the harder will be the rest of winter.

b) The success of the following year's fruit and field crops:
Saying the Lord's Prayer backwards on Christmas Eve insures good farming the next year.

If on Christmas night wine ferments in the barrel, a good wine year will follow.

If the sun shines through the apple tree on Christmas Day, the following year will have an abundant harvest.

If Christmas Day is windy, trees will bear much fruit.

Light Christmas, light wheatsheaf,
Dark Christmas, heavy wheatsheaf.

A clear and bright sun on Christmas Day foretells a peaceful year of plenty.

c) The possiblity of disease and death:
If the wind grows stormy before sunset, it betokenth sickness in the spring and autumn quarters.

A green Christmas makes a fat churchyard.

An interesting variation of the control capabilities of Christmas involves the much sung "Twelve Days of Christmas." According to folklore, the twelve days of

Christmas have jurisdiction over the weather in each of the coming twelve months. No other key day (see page 53) is accredited with possessing this potency necessary to meterologically manipulate more than one particular day or season. However, since Christmas is the climax of the Christian year, its influence is extensive. Simply stated, Christmas makes the almanac for the year.

There is also the unique belief that Christmas weather, turned inside-out, is the weather for Easter Sunday. This theory of opposition is more than likely representative of the obvious: the beginning and ending of the life of Christ. Quite coincidental, though, of all the Christmas folklore forecasts, this group of Christmas-Easter adages verifies as being the most meteorologically accurate. Climatological statistics reveal that if winter is late in sending its seasonal chills, then snow tends to fall much later than is normally expected in spring.

If at Christmas ice hangs on trees,
Clover may be cut at Easter.
A warm Christmas, a cold Easter.
Christmas in snow, Easter in clover
A green Christmas, a white Easter.

Despite the many "If Christmas . . . then Easter" sayings, Easter is not solely dependent on Christmas for its weather lore. The Lenten Season is studded with a plethora of pious predictions pivotal about Easter Sunday, which seems to wander aimlessly from one weekend to the next, never falling on the same date in two consecutive years. Actually, though, there is a pre-planned pattern for determining the annual calendar positioning of Easter. The entire program is reliant on the first full moon to appear after the vernal equinox (first day of spring). For centuries, the full moon has been known as the Paschal Moon. Now, the Sunday immediately following the Paschal Moon is Easter, and forty days (not

SHROVE TUESDAY . . .
"When the sun is shining on Shrove Tuesday, it means well for rye and peas."

ASH WEDNESDAY . . .
"The wind that prevails on Ash Wednesday will remain throughout Lent."

PALM SUNDAY . . .
"A bad Palm Sunday denotes a year of failing crops."

GOOD FRIDAY . . .
"A wet Good Friday means very little hay."

EASTER SUNDAY . . .
"Weather on Easter . . . weather at harvest."
"Pleasant Easter weather indicates a bountiful crop."

PASTER SUNDAY (Sunday after Easter) . . .
"Rain on Paster Sunday means rain on every Sunday until Pentecost."

PENTECOST SUNDAY (seven Sundays after Easter) . . .
"Rain on Pentecost forbodes *evil.*"

counting Sundays) prior to the decided Easter date is Ash Wednesday, the commencement of Lent.

The many movable Easter holidays are shadowed by their faithful forecasts, regardless of the nominal date. It is because of this flexibility and mobility that the group of Easter forecasts receives the lowest accuracy ratings of all the proverbial predictions. However, personal journals do boast of accounts when the entire set of religious renditions, weatherwise, proved to be 100% correct, a percentage figure never equaled, or rumored to be equaled, in the professional offices of modern meteorolgists.

All in all, between the two major Christian holy days of Christmas and Easter, over fifty weather wisdoms are hereto listed. In addition to these, hundreds, and possibly thousands, or other colloquial versions are traceable.

Some silly,
some sincere.
Some are vague,
and some quite clear.

Some are sacred,
some mundane,
Some say snow,
and some say rain.

Read them over,
say they're funny,
Then recall our
Easter bunny.

Are we perfect,
free of flaws.
Don't we watch
for Santa Claus?

Now we're fans
of Mother Nature.
Old Man Winter and Jack Frost
are the ones that we accost
Once, however,
it was Christ
Whom we sought for our advice. *

Calendar of Climatological Clergymen

Sin is "in," and saints just ain't.
Another page has turned.
Ideas that great-grandpa had?
— Forgotten, lost or burned.

Technology and science thrive.
Success is marked by money.
Flourescent lights and indoor heat,
Turn cool-dark days to "sunny."

But yester-year was just a child,
Caressing Dad so tight,
Assured that he would keep us safe,
And teach us wrong from right.

The Saints helped out with daily chores,
And never went "on strike."
Designing lovely flakes of snow;
Creating none alike.

Dropping rain where God prescribed,
Stirring up the wind;
Charting routes for storms to track,
Close-aimed at those who sinned.

It was the saints, (old-timers knew)
Who pulled it all together.
The end result? Their skills combined?
*We still, today, call "weather."**

St. Valentine and St. Patrick are the only two saints here in our country who have managed to perpetuate their popularity to a point where they repeatedly reap respectable revenues for American businesspeople. In commemorative thanks to these two men, their names are specially imprinted on our calendars annually. However, the names of some one to two hundred other less prominent saints go unrecognized by calendar printers and publishers.

It has only been in recent times that the vast legion of saints has dwindled to a puny pious pair. Antiques and artifacts of yesteryear clearly confess of an earlier era when ecclesiastical entities were as well known as today's television stars. People of all age groups were familiar with the sainted men of God and their appointed feast dates, even to the extent of using the holy days in common conversation.

Torn, tattered, and tainted with time-telling yellow, calendars, registers, and almanacs of several hundred years back are interestingly crowded with countless masses, feast days, and church celebrations, reflecting a long gone reign of religion. In contrast, today, bold-typed newspaper headlines read: CHRISTIAN ILLITERATES, and discuss current church catastrophes regarding the religious ignorance of professed believers; e.g., surveys show only two out of every ten "believers" can recall, without reference, three of the Ten Commandments!

Also, much in contrast with twentieth century skepticism, the majority of our forebearers were convinced that God (not color radar) governed the weather, assisted by some of his devoutest devotees. Using the convenience of the already existent spiritual calendar, the weather power of each saint was comfortably matched with his established feast day, incorporated into what became known as the "Saints' Day Weather Calendar."

Confusing as all weather-related items are, though, some of the saint's day weather sayings listed on the summary were totally unrelated to the saint himself. In this case, a certain climatic condition was noted to occur reliably on a particular date, and since holy days held more significance than numerical dates, the weather was spoken of in conjunction with a feast day.

I would like to take this opportunity to express my belated sympathies to the unfortunate men who were persecuted prior to their earthly departure, and then got stuck at random, with some recurring weather phenomenon, destined to be tortured for years post mortem. Such was the case with St. Joseph.

In 1893, a terrible drought prompted a group of irate Italians to heave-ho a huge statue of St. Joseph into a withered, water-thirsty garden so he could see, firsthand, just how critical the crisis was. Checking the Saints' Day Calendar, we do find St. Joseph listed on March 19 with the following weather wisdom:

"If St. Joseph's day clear . . . so follows a fertile year." This saying is backed by neither legend nor circumstance, but even so, it was Joseph that the folks held responsible for the rain shortage and the bum forecast.

Through the ages, countless other saints have been banished from holy places or stood on their heads for punishment, as a result of "expected" conditions, based on the saints' day weather calendar.

Despite the ridicule and ruckus, the Saints' Day Weather Calendar continued to be carefully contemplated and consulted by the commoners until the beginning of the twentieth century. However, because it was oftentimes revered and respected more so than royal directives, it was usually scorned by the agnostic members of the aristocracy. In fact, during the reign of England's Henry VIII, an imperial edict banned all almanacs and/or calendars that mentioned the dogmatic implications pertaining to saints and the weather.

Today, the Saints' Day Weather Calendar is virtually unheard of and its lore, legend, and litany have been forgotten. For the sake of nostalgia, the remainder of this chapter is devoted to that Calendar of Climatological Clergyman, and the semblage of saints it celebrates. Individual chapters to follow will cover Saints Swithin, Luke, Martin, Pancras, Seratius, and Mamertius.

Saint Hilary – January 14:

Logic would lead us to believe that winter's coldest day is the day of the seasonal solstice. On the first day of winter, the hours of darkness far exceed the period of sunlight, with nearly fifteen hours of nighttime "heat loss" and only nine hours to regain solar heat. However, our coldest weather does not usually arrive until mid-January. The technical explanation for this "lag of seasons" involves the protective blanket around our globe, the atmosphere. Regardless of what precise moment the "axis tilt/orbit plane" situation occurs which marks the moment of winter's start, the cumulative heat trapped by clouds and particulants keep the earth from undergoing an abrupt cool-off. Instead, a gradual seepage of warmth occurs, with the effect of our earth's angular change (in relation to the sun), and is not felt for three to five weeks.

It is because of the lag of seasons that St. Hilary's Day

blindly collided with the uncelebrated honor of being the coldest day of the year.

Checking biographical sketches, there seems to be no tie-in whatsoever, between Hilary (the Bishop of Pouters) and weather of any sort. But, year after year, St. Hilary's Day is monitored as being the turning point of winter, with average daily highs on the upswing following the second week of January.

Further verifying the chill associated with the feast day of St. Hilary, we find eight of the fifty states have all-time record low temperatures set on or about the thirteenth of January.

Delaware: —17, January 17, 1893, Millsboro.

Idaho: —60, January 16, 1943, Island Park Dam.

Iowa: —47, January 12, 1912, Washta.

Maryland: —40, January 13, 1912, Oakland.

Massachusetts: —34, January 18, 1957, Birch Hill Dam.

Oklahoma: —37, January 18, 1930, Watts.

Rhode Island: —23, January 11, 1942, Lingston.

South Carolina: —20, January 18, 1977, Caesar's Head.

(Records through 1978, source: NOAA, U.S. Commerce Department.)

The original link between extreme cold and St. Hilary's day dates back to 1205. January 13 marked the start of a lengthy freeze in England that kept Britons shivering the remainder of January, all of February, and most of March. It is said that no thaw occurred for nearly seventy days, with relief coming, at last, on March 22.

Here in our country, St. Hilary's Feast Day corresponded with the annual "rising of the sap" ceremony observed by the northern tribes of the American Indians. Paying special tribute to Nanabozko (the cold weather spirit), the celebration was staged at the yearly commencement of the sap flow in maple trees. In days-of-old, January sap yield was quite common.

St. Sulpice – January 17:

Frost on this day means a good spring.

St. Vincent – January 22:

Sun on St. Vincent's means good wine crops for the next season. Patron saint of winegrowers, St. Vincent of Sargossa is recognized as the most celebrated of Spanish martyrs. Persecuted under Diocletian in 304, St. Vincent was lashed to a grill and roasted while simultaneously being toasted by a glowing-hot iron plate applied to parts of his body untouched by the fire. Despite the terrible torture techniques, Vincent refused to denounce his well-founded faith and was cast into prison to suffer a slow painful death.

It is said that the jailer patrolling Vincent's cell ground was instantly converted to Christianity upon seeing the saint's cell filled with bright light as the near-to-dead saint paced the floor, loudly praising the Lord.

It is the incredible "illuminated prison" incident that underlies the weather maxim associated with Vincent. January in the northern hemisphere is traditionally a month of maximum cloud cover, so any sunlight is unexpected and well appreciated, especially the sunlight of January 22. If the sun appears on the twenty-second, it is viewed as a good-luck sign to vineyard tenders, guaranteeing their crop will grow and flourish under St. Vincent's guardianship.

St. Paul – January 25:

January 25 is the anniversary date of the miraculous conversion of Paul from a fanatic Pharisee to a Christian Apostle. (Paul's feast date is June 29) It is on this conversion date that for centuries Englishmen have sung:

If St. Paul's be fair and clear,
It promises a happy year.
But if it changes to snow or rain,
There will be dear all sorts of grain.
Or if the wind does blow aloft,
Great stirs will vex the world full of oft.

The weather reasoning behind this hymn seems non-existent, but it is agreed that the three portions of this folksong forecast represent the three individual fountains that sprang up at the three spots where Paul's head bounced, following his decapitation, at the site now titled Tre Fontaine (French: three fountains).

Another St. Paul's Day weather expression is:

If Paul's Day is fine,
It will be a fine spring.

St. Bridget – February 1:

Snow on this day indicates full ditches come spring.

St. Dorothy – February 6:

She brings the most snow.

This weather statement differs from the other pious prognostications because it is not prophetic. On the contrary, it is definitive, certainly indicating it is a ditty derived from an analytical survey. Out of X number of years, Y number of times winter's deepest snow was measured on the sixth of February. Statistics support the Dorothy's Day declaration with a reasonable degree of probability. February is the snowiest of all months in the United States and Great Britain.

St. Eulalie – February 12:

If the sun does smile on St. Eulalie's Day
Good apples and cider, they say.

St. Peter (Peter Damian) – February 22:

The night of this day indicates the weather for the next forty days.

St. Matthias – February 24:

If there is ice it will break it,
If no ice, it will make it.

St. Matthias, a companion of Jeus since his baptism, was not one of the original disciples, but later was awarded membership in the Twelve, following the vacancy left by Judas Iscariot.

Only two men were suggested for the great honor of being in the inner group, Matthias and Barsabbas. Matthias won by lot. It is that same chanceable, "if not one, then the other" concept that underlies the weather saying coupled with the feast day of Matthias, February 24.

Regardless of existent weather, good or bad, Matthias Day brings a reversal of conditions. This idea is also captured in the folklore phrase: "Matthias sends sap into the tree."

In order for maple sap to flow freely, a mild, rhythmic temperature fluctuation is required, with afternoon highs climbing 10-15 degrees above freezing, and overnight lows sinking 2-8 degrees below freezing. Sudden warmth or rapid cooling halts the natural pump action within the sugar maple, which is activated by the afore-mentioned temperature readings. It is the cessation of the sap flow, due to the sporadic climatic change characteristic during the last week of February, that forms the basis of the second Matthias day ditty.

St. Romanus – February 28:

St. Romanus bright and clear, augurs a goodly year.

St. David – March 1:

On St. David's Day, put oats and barley in the clay.

St. Winwaloe – March 3:

Winwaloe comes as if he were mad.

March in the northern hemisphere has always been sort of a catch-all month weatherwise, marking the transition between the dreaded dead of winter and the sounds and scents of sensational spring.

During the early portion of the month, nature's anger is apparent in the form of strong howling winds and bitter cold temperatures. As the month progresses, though, weather conditions become more agreeable, until finally March silently surrenders to the less fickle month of April. The religious remark that "Winwaloe comes as if he were mad" is more popularly presented in the pagan proverb: March comes in like a lion (and goes out like a lamb.) This comment is of English ancestry, dating back to the 1600s. It received wide recognition following publication in 1624 of a poem titled "A Wife for a Month," by John Fletcher. Again, the fiercely cold temperatures and raging, roaring winds are what qualifies the beginning of March to be associated with a wild lion.

St. Patrick – March 17:

"The warm side of a stone turns up, and the broad back goose begins to lay."

St. Joseph – March 19:

"St. Joseph's Day clear, so follows a fertile year."

St. Benedict – March 21:

"If it rains on this day, it will rain for forty days."

The Annunciation – March 25:

"A clear St. Mary's Day, a fruitful year ahead."

St. Vincent (Ferrer) – April 5:

"If this day is fair, there will be more water than wine."

St. George – April 23:
"If by this time the rye has grown high enough to hide a crow, a good harvest can be expected."

St. Mark – April 25:
"Rain on this day speaks ill for fruit crops."

St. Jacob – May 1:
"Rain on Jacob's Day, expect a fertile year."

St. Urban – May 25:
"If St. Urban laughs, then the grapes will cry.
If St. Urban cries, then there will be very few grapes."

St. Philip (Neri) – May 26:
"If it rains on St. Philip's Day, the poor will not need help from the rich."

St. Barnabas – June 11:
Rain on St. Barnabas is good for grapes.

St. Vitus – June 15:
"If St. Vitus Day be rainy weather,
It will rain for thirty days together."

St. Vitus is more often mentioned in medical journals than in meteorological memoirs, since chorea, a disease characterized by involuntary muscle contractions, is commonly referred to as St. Vitus's Dance. St. Vitus is the patron saint of comedians, which possibly links him with the weather, or more specifically, TV weather-casters.

St. John – June 24:
There are two surviving saints' day weather sayings concerning John the Baptist. Both are associated with his birthday rather than the date of his final persecution at the end of August.

If it rains on St. John's eve, the filbert nuts will be spoiled.
No crops before St. John's Day are worthy of praising.

Of particular interest, one of the two sayings refers to the night before St. John's birth, St. John's eve, a holiday once celebrated with great outward display. On the twenty-third night in June, residents of many countries observed the sanction of building fires at the town's geographical high point. A quote by Dom L. P. Gueranger states "Scarce had the last rays of the setting sun died away, when all the world over, immense columns of flames arose from every mountain top, and in an instant every town and village and hamlet was lighted up."

Today, only a mere remnant of this glorious custom exists. St. John's Fire is the term applied to heat lightning visible during the last half of June on or about the nativity of St. John.

St. Mary (July 2), St. Martin Bullion (July 4), St. Gallo (July 15), St. Anne (July 26) and St. Godelieve (July 27):

Unlike St. Swithin (See chapter 9), the five saints listed above have all been unfairly paired with wet weather. Examining climatological statistics, though, we do find reason behind this rainy ruckus. Meteorologically, July holds first place honors for being both the month of maximum thunderstorm frequency and the rainiest month. Heat, humidity, and atmospheric instability (the prime requirements for thunderstorm formation) are commonplace in mid-summer. In fact, it is not unusual to hear a large percentage of July forecasts ending in a phrase of uncertainty, like "and the chance of widely scattered afternoon and evening thunderstorms." It is during these thunderstorms that most record-breaking, short-term rainfalls occur, with an incredible 30.7 inches of rain falling in just six hours back on July 17, 1942.

Considering July's preference for precipitation, it is understandable how it came about that Mary, Bullion, Gallo, Anne, and Godelieve all became associated with extended periods of rainy weather.

If it rains on St. Mary's, it will rain for a month straight.

If Martin Bullion's Day brings rain, it will rain for forty days and nights.

Rain on Gallo's day will last for forty days.

Rain on St. Anne's will continue for a month and a week.

Rain on this day will continue for forty days.

St. James – July 25:

Sunshine and rain are the two most popular items mentioned as the governing factors in "control day" forecasts found on the Saints' Weather Calendar. On St. James' Day, though, future weather is dependent on clouds. The maxim states: "Puffy white clouds on this day foretell much snow in the coming winter."

Why it is that James, and only James, is associated with "puffy white clouds" is not recorded with any sense of surety. Therefore, I will present two logical assumptions and subsequent explanations for the rare occurrence.

First off, in art, James is emblematically represented by a scallop shell, in remembrance of his fisherman profession before being called by Christ. It is possible that the series of curves (typical in the appearance of cumulus clouds) was thought by ancients to resemble the formation of a cockleshell.

A more meteorological analysis as to why the cumulus cloud is linked to St. James involves the nickname used by Jesus in addressing both James and John. Because of their impetuous natures, Christ called the brothers *boanerges* which is by translation *sons of thunder*. This surname is believed to have been first instituted as the result of the holy group being discriminated against on their final journey to Jerusalem. Enraged against the residents of the Samaritan village that refused them lodging, James and John asked Jesus: (Luke 9:54)

"Master, shall we order fire down from heaven to burn them up?" Similar to the occasional flare-up of James' temper, the docile, unsuspecting, fair weather cumulus clouds sometimes grow out of control, developing into an ugly fierce storm cloud technically known as the cumulonimbus (CB) (more popularly termed a *thunderhead*.)

Another weather prediction based on the feast day of St. James is:

"When it is fair three Sundays after St. James,
It betokenth that corn shall be very good.
But if it rains, then the corn withereth."
(from 67 *Farmer's Almanac*)

In this prognosis, the three Sundays are representative of the three figures viewed by James at the Transfiguration, Moses, Elijah and Christ.

Other lore associated with the feast of St. James:

Rain before noon . . . winter before Christmas
Rain after noon . . . winter after Christmas

Sunshine on St. James betokens of cold weather.
Rain on St. James betokens of warm moist weather.

St. Lawrence – August 10:

"Fine weather on this day indicates a good autumn."

If the fine weather desired on St. Lawrence Day continues through the night, one might catch a glimpse of St. Lawrence's tears. The "tears" of St. Lawrence are the shooting stars belonging to the Perseid meteor shower which reaches its peak in activity on the feast day of St. Lawrence. This reference is traceable back more than 1,000 years.

St. Bartholomew – August 24:
Bartholomew brings the cold dew.

St. Matthew – September 21:
"Matthew's day, bright and clear,
Brings good wine in the next year."

St. Michael – September 29:
As many days old as the moon is on Michaelmas,
So many floods thereafter.
Many acorns on Michaelmas . . .
A hard winter will come to pass.

St. Gallus – October 16:
No rain on Gallus, a dry spring will follow.

St. Simon – October 28:
"St. Simon is never dry."

It's difficult to believe an expression like this one regarding St. Simon unless you're familiar with a similar legend. Such a legend exists too. Rain Day is alive and living in the United States in a small town named Waynesburg, in the southwest corner of Pennsylvania. Each year since 1876, a new hat has been wagered against a local or national celebrity betting that it would rain. As of 1980, (July 29) Rain Day has exhibited an amazing 87½% accuracy level with rain falling ninety-one out of 104 years. Hence . . . "It always rains on Rain Day."

St. Catherine (of Alexandria) - November 25:
"Weather on St. Catherine's Day, so will February be."

This is one of the more mysterious of saint day weather sayings, with Saint Catherine Day deemed responsible for the future weather of an entire month for no known reason.

What is recorded, though, weatherwise, about the beautiful maiden concerns her martyrdom. Her body was to be broken on a spiked wheel but, during the final preparation, a bolt of lightning struck and destroyed the wheel, and Catherine was saved. As a result, the 200 soldiers who witnessed the miraculous event were immediately converted. Unfortunately, all the new converts were soon beheaded, along with the spared saint.

St. Andrew – November 30:

Andrew's snow is bad for corn and wheat.

St. Thomas – December 21:

"St. Thomas always will be gray;
The longest night and shortest day."

December 21 marks the winter solstice and as the saying claims, it is on this date that the nighttime hours far exceed the hours of day.

St. Stephen – December 26:

Wind on St. Stephen's Day foretells of bad grapes the following year.

Innocents' Day – December 28:

"A bright day of plenty
A dark, wet day, a year of scarcity."

Other religious holy days that have been haphazardly traced to weather lore for centuries include:

All Fool's Day — April 1:

"If it thunders on All Fool's Day,
'Twill bring good crops of corn and hay."

All Saints' Day — November 1:

If the beech acorn is wet on this day,
So will the winter be wet.

Houses of Heavenly Hosts

A cloud is just a puff of stuff
It holds no shape or form,
It might drift by without a sound,
Or house a violent storm.

Like people, every cloud's unique,
Some disappoint, some please us.
We look at some, find nothing new . . .
Yet sometimes we see Jesus!

Strange beasts we sometimes see, perhaps,
(An elephant or lion)
Or maybe view a quaint ole town,
Or golden, gleaming Zion.

A play it is, produced by God,
With new scenes all the time.
With Broadway skill the clouds all act,
Their sky-staged pantomime.

No tickets sold; just join the crowd,
And gaze up at the sky
No reruns, no commercial ads . . .
A pleasure you can't buy. *

It could be said that a cloud holds no shape or form because there are no bones about it, and, *no bones about it* it is the very essence of clouds that easily and logically allows them to be associated with the supernatural. Elusive and ephemeral, clouds are in constant gyration and transformation. Some clouds are graceful, ghost-like drifters, yet other clouds are liverish spirit-sprinters. Capable of worrying and warning, delighting and dazzling, clouds are both magestic and mysterious.

In brief, clouds are *heavenly.* The best living, literary example of this statement is the near-to-synonymous meanings of the "mod" expressions "I'm in seventh heaven" and "I'm up on cloud nine." Both phrases denote a similar feeling of ecstasy, or euphoria; however, one's origin can be traced to religion, whereas the other was born in a weather office.

Being aware of the Scripturally inferred dimensions of heaven (1,500 miles in each direction . . . Revelation 21:16), many sects contend that the *hereafter* is multi-floored, vertically divided into seven separate levels. Each level, in upward ascension, is a more preferred place to spend forever, with the highest level "seventh heaven" the location of elation. There is no greater happiness to be found than in seventh heaven, the expected abode of God, the Most High. No danger, no fear, only jubilation.

Likewise, no danger or fear is found on top of cloud nine. Higher than any other cloud form, the cloud designated "cloud nine" is the cumulonimbus cloud, more commonly known as the *thunderhead.* Inside cloud nine, all sorts of disastrous weather events are occurring; severe up-and-downdrafts, lightning flashes, rain, snow, hail . . . *but* atop the characteristic *anvil,* (sheared off by the high-speed, upper-winds) all is peaceful and sunny.

There is a reason WHY cloud nine is a nine, in lieu of some other number: Clouds are divided into three basic classes (low, mid and high) and each class, in turn, is subdivided into nine types. The ninth member of the low class is the cumulonimbus, or thunderhead, which matures vertically to heights far in excess of other clouds. Also, it is grouped in the low class due to its relatively low base of less than 8,000 feet. Belonging to a special numerical coding system universally understood by weatherpersons, if a nine appears in its proper sequence, it is deciphered as "low cloud nine," (the thunderhead) and is symbolically represented on weather charts as seen below:

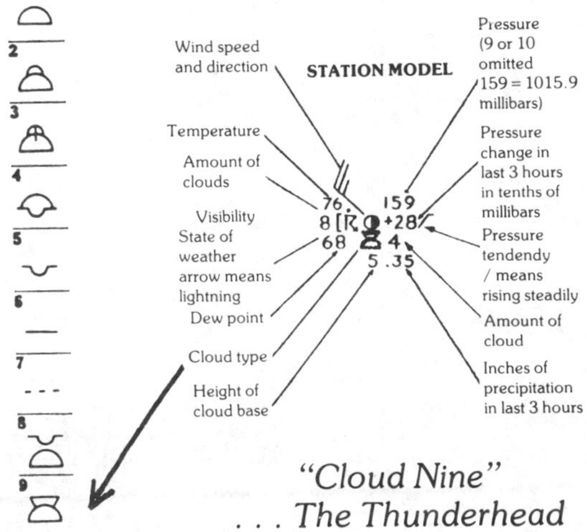

"Cloud Nine"
. . . The Thunderhead

Towering above all other clouds, cloud nine is right up there in seventh heaven. Because of the extreme altitude, earthly problems are invisible to "out-of-this-world" places like cloud nine and seventh heaven.

Aside from the weather-religion relation between cloud nine and seventh heaven, there are only a few other faint traces that reflect the important role clouds played in the lives of our biblical brothers. One of these references is to Abraham's Tree. Abraham's Tree is a sky assemblage consisting of very high, leaf-like cirrus clouds that radiate or "branch out" from a single horizon-point. The title is in remembrance of the most holy of family lineages, the family tree of Abraham, whose limbs branch out as recounted in Matthew 1:1-16. Technically speaking, Abraham's Tree is a cloud formation entitled *cirrus radiatus*.

Jacob's Ladder is another type of phenomenon with religious connotations. Appearing as alternating light and dark bands of sunlight, the effect is caused by solar rays shining through breaks or holes in clouds into a dusty atmosphere. Because this oddity alludes to connect heaven and earth, it's often likened to the heavenly ladder Jacob envisioned. (Genesis 28:12)

The scant remains of clouds with religious roots is indicative of just how our attitude toward clouds has undergone a rotten revision over the last few centuries. In fact, isn't it true that today we most often see and hear about clouds when they're being compared to . . . toilet tissue? Yesteryear clouds were revered and respected, cherished and canonized. They were viewed as houses of heavenly hosts, and the Bible substantiates that theory.

Among those spiritual beings reported as dwelling in clouds is God. Guiding the Israelites through the wilderness, "The Lord went before them by day in a pillar of a cloud" . . . "and took not away the pillar of cloud." (Exodus 13:21-22 KJV)

Incomprehensible, and therefore, inexplicable, laboratory meteorologists often degrade and discount the numerous Scriptural references to a pillar cloud. Nephologists (cloud specialists) ascertain the life expectancy of any one cloud is mere minutes. A cloud formation of a forty-year endurance is *scientifically* impossible. Similarly impossible is the idea of a cloud remaining confined to a limited area for forty years. Even if a cloud were to celebrate forty birthdays, it would soon journey out of the viewing range of the original observers. Noticing the average velocities in the table below, a cloud traveling at the lowest speed of 18 mph would only take four and one half days to track over a 2,000 mile path.

Cloud	Heights (feet)	Average Velocities (miles per hour) Summer	Winter
Cirrus	10,000-50,000	55	70
Cirro-stratus	15,000-45,000	50	65
Mackerel Sky	8,000-36,000	40	55
Alto-cumulus	2,700-27,000	30	40
Nimbus	200-18,000	25	35
Stratus	400-6,000	18	25
Thunderhead	2,500	40	50
Cumulus	2,500	18	25
Fog	Earth's Surface	——	——

Even the capsule description *pillar* is peculiar to contemporary cloud descriptions. The professional cloud observers handbook, the International Cloud Atlas, contains hundreds of characteristic cloud shapes and sizes, yet the only cloud approximating a *vertical upright* is that cloud associated with tornadic activity, the funnel cloud. It is doubtful that *pillar* and *funnel* were two terms used interchangeably, though, since no mention is made of violent circular winds swirling about the guiding phenomenon that led the Israelites.

The erratic path of tornadoes has been successfully compared with the roundabout travels of the chosen people. Tornadoes frequently meander on an indecisive track, hovering at times before advancing onward, quite similar to the character of the pillar cloud. The analogy is discredited, though, by comparing the pillar cloud's longevity to the average survival time of a tornado, reported at only fifteen minutes. The *record* life of a tornado is seven hours, a bit short of forty years.

Using today's scientific standards, sureties, and specifications, the pillar cloud (as biblically referenced over thirty times) was nonexistent.

But, the pillar cloud did exist. Granted, it was not an ordinary cloud of usual demeanor or dimension. It was a cloud of extraordinary, perhaps even "miraculous," appearance. An entire nation would not confidently pursue an inconspicious, commonplace cloud, especially for the time span of the wilderness wanderings. The pillar cloud must have possessed a magnetic-like quality, giving it the ability to attract.

The irresistible magnetism of the pillar cloud was due in part to the fact that occasionally "within the guiding cloud, there appeared the awesome glory of Jehovah." (Exodus 16:10) Strangely enough, though, it is this recurrent divine apparition that links, rather than separates, the pillar cloud from other clouds enumerated on in the Bible. The pillar cloud was never again sighted following the Israelites' entrance into the land of "milk and honey," however, clouds of more normal appearance continue to echo voices of ecclesiastical entities right through the Good Book's end. (See concordance.)

It is not to be insinuated that all biblical references pertain to extraordinary clouds containing heavenly heroes. Bible authors were not ignorant of the scientific status of clouds. In fact, scriptural subjects were aware of and accurately verbose in the more normal formation, function and composition of clouds. This is apparent in the following biblical extracts:

> *He loads the clouds with moisture and they send forth his lightning.* (Elihu . . . Job 37:11)

As a hot, dry land is cooled by clouds . . . (Isaiah 25:5)
He wraps the rain in his thick clouds and the clouds are not split by the weight. (Job 26:8)
"When you see clouds beginning to form in the west, you say, 'Here comes a shower.' And you are right." (Jesus . . . Luke 12:54)

Despite well-founded wisdom concerning the meteorological aspects of clouds, the ancients continued to faithfully fathom the suspended moisture masses in hopes of again finding evidence of celestial creatures as their ancestors had described. Gradually, though, cloud watchers became a much mocked minority, consisting mostly of children, senior citizens, and social "odd-balls." Emphasis was shifted from personal cloud-gazing, to sky-scanning with sophisticated instruments. Expensive equipment punctured, probed, and penetrated clouds and found no tangible traces of anything heavenly. Therefore, the possibility of resident angels, aloft, was officially ruled out.

Sporadically, someone will rekindle an interest in watching the clouds by delivering a moving testimonial of their having seen a Christ-like apparition while looking upward. Unfortunately, although the viewer's faith is permanently reaffirmed, even the closest of friends are silently skeptical, unless *positive* evidence is presented. But, since clouds have no fossils or fingerprints, or dental records, indepth investigations are impossible, so cloud testimonials are tagged "visionary."

Even if a cloud's contour is captured by a quick-minded cameraman, exhibited photographs receive minimal credibility. Non-religionists hasten to discuss trick photography methods and imagery projection, featuring famed farces like *King Kong, The Lost World,* . . . the Cockroach That Swallowed Chicago, etc.

Many snapshots depicting curious cloud-countenances are in existence. These natural, untouched, "untricked" photographs are usually in the treasured possession of the families in which they originated. One such photo was reproduced in the *Marion Star* (Friday, April 14, 1978) before being retired to its owner's heirlooms. This "shot" was photographed by Terry Dodds, using an inexpensive Yashica instant camera. The location is the Smoky Mountains in 1976. A haphazard glance at the view depicts nothing extraordinary. However, a prayerful perusal of the same skyline reveals the semblance of Christ's head, seen as if he were lying in a prone position. Incredibly inspirational, lawmakers in the Ohio Congress have asked for 150 prints of the picture.

In conclusion, at Conclusion . . .
On the Judgment Day,

Don't you wanna be among
The crowds to shout "hurray"?

Don't you wanna see our Christ,
When He first returns,
Don't you wanna hear the horns,
Before the whole world burns?

If you haven't read **The Book,**
You'll not know what to do . . .
Will the Lord come boat or bus?
Or jet flight fifty-two?

Will some chauffeured limousine
Drive up . . . drop off the King?
It's . . . in a CLOUD, the Bible says,
That will from heaven bring.

"The peoples of the earth shall see
Me coming in a cloud" . . .
Those words, a promise, now so old, . . .
Christ spoke them clear and proud.

So keep your eyeballs "peeled," friend,
And do not be surprised, . . .
When someday if it's overcast, . . .
*The SON gets in your eyes . . .!**

A Collection of Cloud Confidants

"When woolly fleeces spread the heavenly way,
No rain, be sure, disturbs the summer's day."

"Hen scratches and filly tails,
Get ready to reef up your top sails."

"Mares tails, mares tails,
Make lofty ships carry low sails."

"When clouds appear like rocks and towers,
The earth's refreshed by frequent showers."

"Be still sad heart, and cease repining,
Behind the clouds is the sun still shining."
Longfellow

Different Strokes

When I was just a little girl,
My grandma said "Don't cry,
It's just the angels beating drums,
A-way up in the sky."

As lightning flashed, my tears leaked out,
Despite what Grandma said . . .
But scenes of marchers robed in white
Paraded through my head.

So many years have passed since then,
And taller now I stand.
Those storms are not as fearful now,
Since Grandma's joined that band.

Today I watch the skies with hope,
As dark clouds roll in fast.
Assured God's drummers will rehearse.
Until the final "blasts."

And when the heavenly trumpet blares,
The Major will descend —
The Judgment Day Pass-in-Review;
The Saints come marchin' in. *
. . . to you, Grandma.

An immunity for *keraunophobia*[1], the fear of thunderstorms, has been pursued for centuries. Countless ages have passed since the intense search first began, but little progress has been made. Persons of all races and ranks have collaborated in the constant probe for something, anything that might prevent, divert, abate, or dissipate the evils of nature's electrical storms. Numerous remedies, ranging from ridiculous to resolute, have been suggested and sampled over the years. Strangely enough, those items which seemed least likely to prove fail-safe were seemingly effective.

The ancient Greeks and Romans regarded the laurel (also known as the bay tree) as an effective antidote against lightning. Laurel leaves, wreathed and worn as amulets, were sported by commoners and dignitaries alike. The most famed for the fad was Tiberius Claudius Nero Caesar who reigned during the time of Christ (A.D. 14-37). In art, Tiberius is seldom seen without his crutch against lightning, and evidently was never forced to learn the fatal lesson taught to Vicomereatus. (According to Sir Thomas Brown's *Vulgar Errors,* Vicomereatus was struck by lightning while wearing his "foil of foliage," and consequently forever put to "rest on his laurels.")

The Germans and French of yesteryear relied on a plant known as St. John's Wort for protection against lightning. Unlike the laurel, St. John's Wort was not a personal safeguard worn by an individual. Instead, annually, on the feast day of St. John (December 27), the plant was gathered, blessed, and then hung in the

---

1. *Keraunos* — Greek word for "thunderbolt".

windows of vulnerable dwellings.

It is interesting to note, at this point, the relation between St. John (the Divine) and the lightning antagonist, St. John's Wort. In Mark 3:17 (RSV) reference is made to a unique nickname, *Boanerges,* used by Jesus to address James and John. Interpreted as *The Sons of Thunder,* it is assumed the brothers earned this title on the road to Jerusalem (Luke 9:54), when they requested Jesus to "consume with lightning" those who rejected their mission. Jesus rebuked the brothers for their proposal, but undoubtedly he was pleased by their defense on his behalf, awarding them the affective appellation.

An array of fire festivals, originating in medieval Europe, were once celebrated in belief that the burning of wood offered future protection from lightning — Easter Eve fires were widespread, especially through the Germanic countries. Saturday night, before Easter, townspeople assembled on pre-designated hilltops (known as Easter Mountains), bringing with them sticks of oak, walnut, or beech to char in consecrated bonfires. Following the religious event, the singed sticks were taken home and re-burned in fireplaces as family members prayed for protection against severe weather.

The traditional family gathering around a blazing hearth on Christmas Eve is also a ritual that once was performed to ward off lightning. The Yule Log, a timber block used as the foundation of the ceremonial fire, was *by necessity* oak wood because of the known fact that lightning had a special preference for oak trees. Each night during the Twelfth-tide, the Yule log was lit. After the Christmas season, its remains were kept handy to burn again, in case of thunderstorms. Oldsters were convinced lightning would not strike while a yule log smoldered.

There are also a few other Christmas "what-nots" associated with lightning: Mistletoe was once suspected to be the result of lightning, growing only where a stroke had touched the ground. And . . . two of our favorite reindeer, Donner and Blitzen, possess names which, when translated from German, mean thunder and lightning! (*Donner* — thunder; *Blitzen* — lightning)

Another article believed to be important in the prevention of lightning strikes was *Christ's Letter*. According to a pamphlet authored by John Leigh in 1835, *Christ's Letter* was a sacred manuscript faithfully carried by keraunophobiacs to avert thunderbolts. (From *Directions for Insuring Personal Safety During Storms of Thunder and Lightning and for the Right Application of Conductors to Houses and Other Buildings*)

Ringing of the Hallowed Bell was a community service performed by the local churches of yesteryear in an effort to detour lightning from the houses of its parishioners. Believed to "break the air" with loud bell-clanging, the method proved to be very effective in achieving its purpose. Unfortunately, because of the height and isolation of church steeples, the practice became extremely unpopular among the bell-ringers, with 103 tollers killed during a thirty-three year period in the mid 1700s (. . . talk about occupational hazards.)

The beautiful fourth century maiden, Barabara Dioscorus, is the patroness for protection against thunder, lightning, and fire. The story behind her sainthood is of interest to any weather buff:

> *Barabara's conversion to Christianity triggered a rage of disapproval on the part of her overly protective father. Consequently, he insisted she renounce her faith or die. Barabara maintained allegiance to her Christian beliefs, despite his numerous threats and tortures, and was eventually put to death (beheaded) at the order of her dad. At the exact moment of her martyrdom, her cruel father was struck outright and killed by a lone lightning bolt. Needless to say, her*

contemporaries were dismayed, and thereby, were convinced Barabara possessed some "power" over controlling "the elements."

Not too long ago, the guardianship of Saint Barabara was respected by even the highest ranking military officials of our country. In fact, D. S. Halacy, Jr., (author of The Weather Changers) reports that "As late as 1940, a portrait of Saint Barabara hung in the office of the Chief of the U.S. Navy Bureau of Ordinance in Washington, D.C." Perhaps the saint's added auspices were deemed necessary following the destruction of the Navy's largest ammunition depot on July 10, 1926; killing sixteen persons and spreading debris across an area of twenty-two statute miles, one lightning bolt targeted Lake Denemark, New Jersey, and caused $79 million worth of damage!

Veneration of storm combatants stems from the fact that lightning and thunder have always been considered the properties of the most divine, supernatural being(s). Zeus, father of Grecian mythological gods, was believed to be the controller of thunderbolts during that empire's heyday. Roman legends ascribed governing power of lightning was at the discretion of Thor (the thunderer), from whence comes our name for the weekday "Thor's Day," better known as Thursday.

The unpredictability of when and where a lightning bolt will strike has always assured humankind that lightning, and its audible accomplice, are a godsend. Hundreds of diverse religions, including Christianity, are in accordance with this assumption.

The Bible frequently alludes to thunder as "the tremendous voice of his majesty." (Job 37:4b) In Exodus 19:9, God informs Moses, he intends on making a personal appearance, in the form of a dark cloud, atop Mt.Sinai. The main purpose of the event is "so that the people themselves can hear me." Later in the same scriptural account, we read "Moses spoke, and God thundered his reply." (vs. 19)

Today, thousands of years following the Mt. Sinai incident, people still react to thunder in the same way the ancients did, "shaking with fear." (Exodus 20:18) Regardless of spiritual commitment, the sudden explosion of thunder instills terror into the hearts of men as well as mice. Why? Because, "it is His voice that echoes in the thunder" of the storm clouds, and like toddlers, we shudder at the stern, demanding voice of our Dad.

Lightning is biblically presented as one of the primary weapons in the Lord's heaven-based arsenal. Each bolt is cautiously dispensed and directed toward a specific, predetermined bull's eye, despite reports we read and hear claiming lightning discharges haphazardly and strikes random locations.

The Old Testament speaks of several godly men who were aided in their missions by timely lightning strikes. Twice, Elijah was able to resist arrest, and prove God's omnipotence, by prayerfully summoning the Lord to "let fire come down from heaven and destroy" his foes. (2 Kings 1:10) David, too, relates how "he flashed fearful arrows of lightning and routed all my enemies." (Psalm 18:14) And, one of the ten plagues Moses demonstrated against Egypt involved God's control over lightning, thunder, hail, and rain.

Repeated scientific experiments have been undertaken in an effort to logically explain, and thereby lessen, the magnificence of lightning. However, as quoted from the *Handbook of Unusual Natural Phenomenon*, "Terrestrial laboratories cannot duplicate nature in all of lightning's idiosyncrasies; just as terrestrial theorists cannot explain all of lightning's quirks." Outstanding among the inexplicable lightning rarities are *lightning from a clear sky* and *ball lightning*.

In particular, ball lightning is recognized as the most

incredible form of lightning. For years, its existence was bluntly denied by intellectuals, with witnesses to the phenomena tagged as "illusionists." Recently, though, the Atmospheric Science Research Center (ASRC) in Albany, New York, has admitted that ball lightning is real, although "not a clearly definable act of nature."

Round, oval, or pear-shaped in appearance, ball lightning is noted to spin as it either hovers in places or tracks an erratic horizontal path. It has an uncanny fondness for sneaking indoors through cracks and crevices and usually terminates with an explosive "pop" following a brief life span of one to eight seconds. Unlike the other, more familiar varieties of lightning (sheet, ribbon, forked, heat), ball lightning seldom harms anyone, a specialty that links it with St. Elmo's Fire.

The appellation, "St. Elmo's Fire," is given to a glowing display of static electricity, usually concentrated around a high-pointed object, such as a ship's mast or a church steeple. The color in the electrified "cloud" is blue, blue-green or green, and is considered a visible sign of divine guardianship by St. Elmo, the patron saint of sailors.

Elmo is an Italian corruption of the Lebanese name of Erasmus. Erasmus was a bishop and hermit of Lebanon, and is associated with seamanship for a most peculiar, *gross* reason. Legend states that the method used for his death-torture was "winding his intestines out of his body, onto a windlass"! A windlass and a ship's capstan are both objects used to wind rope, so sailors "identified" with Elmo's death-device, and adopted Elmo as their special saint.

While St. Elmo's Fire is being observed, danger is not imminent. This concept is verified by the fact that records tell of no destruction ever caused by "Elmo's glow." However, the presence of the phenomena does visibly suggest that the atmosphere is "primed" for thunderstorm activity. Elmo's glow is interpreted as an omen of severe weather to come. The belief is that the Saint provides ample time for the seafarers to "batten down the hatches."

Last night I saw St. Elmo's stars
with their glittering lanterns all at play,
On tops of the masts and tips of the spars
And I knew we should have foul weather today.

Another oddity that places ball lightning and St. Elmo's Fire into partnership is their possible participation in biblical history. Some scholars speculate it was either ball lightning or Elmo's glow that illuminated the shrub from which an angel spoke to Moses. It is written,

> *"And the angel of the Lord appeared unto him in a flame of fire out of the midst of a bush: and he looked, and behold, the bush burned with fire, and the bush was not consumed."* (Exodus 3:2 KJV)

Though the mystery of the burning bush deserves to retain its rating as "miraculous," the scriptural account does, in some ways, parallel other descriptive summaries of the two rare lightning types, ball lightning and St. Elmo's Fire.

Lightning exemplifies God's omnipotence and omnipresence. Striking eight and one-half million times each day, lightning has been observed at all geographical locations. It heats the air as it travels through to a temperature four times as hot as the sun. Annually, in the United States alone, lightning is the cause of $100 million damage. Each single bolt contains an average current of 30,000 amperes and delivers to the earth energy equivalent to what all our country's electric power plants are producing during the same amount of time.

"He fills his hands with lightning bolts. He hurls each at its target. We feel his presence in the thunder. May all sinners be warned." (Job 36: 32, 33)

Thunder and Lightning Lore

According to the Maryland Folklore Archives, "Thunder is God dragging trunks around in his attic."

Thunder in the morning,
All day storming . . .
Thunder at night,
Traveler's delight.

Thunder in the spring, cold will bring.

Thunder at morn, wind is born.
Thunder at noon, rain comes soon.

Thunder at eve, a tempest will weave.

. . . Thunder in February frightens maple sap back in the ground.

Yaller gal, yaller gal, flashin' through the night,
Summer storms will pass you by, unless the lightning's white.

Lightning in the south, brings little else but drought.

Do not sew on Ascension Day or lightning will strike close by.

Thunders of the Vatican: The anathemas and denunciations of the Pope.

Lightning-rod Roy: Roy C. "Dooms" Sullivan, a retired ranger in Virginia's Shenandoah National Park, has been struck by lightning SEVEN times, a Guiness World Record few strive to equal.

How far is the lightning? Upon seeing a lightning flash, begin counting "Chimpanzees," until you hear the thunder. Divide the number of chimpanzees by five. The answer will be the distance, in miles, to the strike site. (Any word taking one second to say can be used.)

Pennies from Heaven (and other loose change)

Don't waste all your "bread,"
'Cuz someday you'll "knead dough."
Save pennies from heaven,
And pay what you owe.

A rainy day's comin'.
(Don't say I'm "all wet.")
Misfortune is yours if
With God you're in debt.

So pay back his love,
And his interest receive:
A share of his wealth waits,
For all who believe. *

I remember gazing at the sky a lot as a young child. I expected something to fall — not just any old something either. I expected money. Daily I listened to Pat Boone sing his "Pennies from Heaven" song, and I believed it, sincerely. Faced with both a financial predicament and a numismatist's interest in *foreign* currency, I waited and watched for many years. Finally, when I was in the second semester of high school economics, the myths of my childhood were shattered as I was forced to accept the fact that a penny wasn't heaven sent, despite the fact each one read "In God We Trust."

A decade or so later, my earnest concern for pennies from heaven was reinstated when I carefully perused the Bible and stumbled over the following verse: "He will open to you his wonderful treasury of rain in the heavens." (Deuteronomy 28:12) Aha! I knew it! There are *fog banks* and *snow banks* and there just had to be a *treasury* of rain because "everytime it rains, it rains pennies from heaven."

Precipitation is a valuable commodity. Admittedly, raindrops aren't pre-stamped with face values as I had earlier envisioned, but each drop is worth a "pretty penny." Besides providing priceless moisture for thirsty plants, rainwater is responsible for transferring vital nutrients from the air into the soil. Nitrogen and oxygen, in particular, are chemically combined aloft under the intense heat of lightning, and rely on rainwater to wash the newly formed oxide into the ground. Literally, tons of this fertilizer are showered on the acreage of the United States annually, nourishing plants and greening the grass. In recognition of rain's beneficial contributions, farmers in Illinois refer to a heavy downpour as a "million dollar" rain.

Snow is also a worthy product. First analyzed in 1852, snow contains nitrates, sulphates, calcium, and potassium, the basic components of fertilzer. Because it is packed with these soil enrichers, an average winter's snowfall in the Central Plains is estimated to be worth $20 per acre. Centuries earlier, Frenchmen expressed this same idea in the saying "a proper February snowfall is worth a pile of manure." (My sentiments exactly when

I'm stranded in a roadside drift.)

Unlike snow and rain, hail is NOT among the treasures hidden in the angel-guarded depository of heaven. Instead, hail is a weather-weapon, secured in the Lord's arsenal, ready for quick access at his decision to stage an assault on earthlings.

Actually, a hailstone is a raindrop that's been on one "hail" of a trip. It spends its infancy as a tiny water droplet amidst a developing cumuliform cloud, then soon after it earns its "rain" classification, it's hijacked by a forceful updraft and begins to solidify in the upper levels of its parent cumulonimbus cloud. Next, the young iceball is snatched by an anxious downdraft and ushered back below the feezing level, where partial thawing occurs. The process continues. Up, down; freeze, melt; until, at last, the hailstone is hurled out of the vicious cloud.

Property damage resulting from hail far exceeds the destruction brought about by all the tornadoes. Appraisers estimate that, each year, hail causes monetary losses amounting to around $315 million dollars, with the bulk of the deficit claimed by farmers, angry farmers who scornfully refer to hail as the "white plague."

The idea of calling hail a plague is certainly not newfangled. Documented in the early chapters of Exodus, hail was one of the original ten plagues that God inflicted on Egypt prior to Israel being dismissed from bondage. The Lord vowed to Moses: "I am going to send a plague . . . I will send a hailstorm across the nation such as there has never been since Egypt was founded." The affliction materialized as promised . . . "and the Lord sent thunder and hail and lightning. All Egypt lay in ruins. Everything left in the fields, men and animals alike, was killed, and the trees were shattered and the crops were destroyed." (Exodus 9:14-25)

In today's world, reports of human demise due to hail are unheard of; however, reliable sources from yesteryear are interspersed with accounts of such fatal instances. As recently as 1936, nineteen Baralong tribesmen were killed by a thirty-minute hailstorm that pelted a native area of the Union of South Africa. And, forty-eight years earlier (April 30, 1888), the most murderous hailstorm of modern times left 246 persons dead in the Morababad District of northern India. Even here, in the United States, death due to hail *has* occurred, with the last incident happening on the thirteenth of May in 1930 when a farmhand, working in a field 30 miles northwest of Lubbock, Texas, was stoned to death by a fall of hailstones the size of grapefruits.

Deadly hailstones the size of grapefruits develop and drop only during the severest of thunderstorms. Normally, hailstones grow no larger than three-quarters of an inch in diameter and are incapable of being cause to human expiration. Larger, heavier hailstones *do* pose a constant threat to us though, and one study group has already prepared a risk potential plan for the public, summarizing our chances of ever encountering odd-size, brutal hail. From this investigation, we learn that only one out of every 800 thunderstorms produces hail the size of walnuts. And, for sports fans, baseball-size hail is pitched earthward only once in every 5,000 thunderstorms. Considering these statistics, chances are next-to-nill that anyone of us will ever have to dodge an eighty-pound hailstone like the townfolk of Salina, New Mexico, did back in 1888. However, we must not be too confident. The aforementioned statistical analysis does not make provisions for the great hailstorm predicted for the latter part of the Tribulation Period.

The day is fast approaching when we will see a new breed of hailstones, iceballs from heaven weighing a talent (137 pounds). These huge hunks of hail will bombard the earth and cause massive destruction in both property and life and "they will curse God because of the terrible hail." (Revelation 16:21)

Besides the usual elements expected to descend from

the clouds (like rain, snow and hail), occasionally we're greeted by other pieces of peculiar precipitation. In the last one hundred years alone, it has "rained" fish and eels, frogs and toads, worms and snakes, spider webs and hazel nuts, and, of course, cats and dogs. Strangely enough, of all the items listed above, the only two NOT officially observed and recorded in the annals of weather history are the two we hear of most frequently, cats and dogs. Considered a cliche as early as 1738, the colloquial expression, "it's raining cats and dogs," is an offshoot of Norse mythology: Rain is symbolized by the cat (an animal believed to have great forecasting wisdom), and the wind is represented by a dog, the faithful attendant of the Norse storm-god, Odin. Properly used, the familiar climatological clause refers to a heavy rain with accompanying winds.

Tornadoes and waterspouts are the meteorological mechanisms most often accused of causing weird weather "falls." These whirling columns of air are characterized by their violent, uplifting currents and therefore are suspected of sucking up objects from one area and later showering them out, miles away from their homesite. To naive news reporters, the explanation is satisfactory. However, the inquisitive individual questions the authenticity of such a statement since, in each instance, only one specific article is "dumped" when the non-destructive cyclonic storm passes. Why? No one knows for sure.

Scientists may never be able to adequately resolve all the documented cases of falling material. Many accounts simply deny systematic reasoning, and best conform to the works of the supernatural. A prime example of a supernaturalistic rainfall is described in Exodus 16:4-13. In this biblical account, we find the people of Israel longing for edible meat. Acting in response to their complaints, God plans, predicts, and proceeds to "rain down food from heaven" in the form of an anomalous "rain of quail." The second time the Israelites lust for meat, again "the Lord sent a wind that brought quail from the sea, and let them fall into the camp and all around it . . ." 2 cubits high.[1] (Numbers 11:31) These two "fowl weather" episodes, though nearly three thousand years old, are surprisingly concurrent with more recent reports of "rare rains," many of which are described in *The Handbook of Unusual Natural Phenomenon*, by William R. Corliss, 1977.

To detect all sundry sorts of prominent precipitation, the weathercaster utilizes an expensive piece of electronic equipment called "radar." Radar consists of a transmitter that emits high-frequency radio waves and a receiver that absorbs the waves after they've been reflected off of hydrometeors.[2] Over the past thirty years, the radar unit has proved to be an invaluable aid to forecasters. Its ability to scan the skies has provided weatherfolk with the information necessary to precisely prewarn the public of approaching weather dangers.

Because of weather-radar's diversified "talents," forecasters have learned, not only to rely on, but to revere radar as if it were some sort of god. Finding this neo-religion competitively clever, the news media have eagerly promoted radar, ceremoniously presenting it to the public via daily television broadcasts. Using photographic "magic" (not unlike that practiced by the Wizard of Oz), most stations have filmed, then enlarged their saucer-size radar scope until the artless piece of equipment has been transformed into a colossal contrivance, dwarfing the duty weathercaster, and demanding audience submission.

It is virtually impossible to ignore weather radar. From coast to coast, it now seems to be a mandatory requirement for each and every TV weathercaster to

---

1. 1 cubit equals 18-22 inches.
2. Hydrometeors compose all forms of precipitation.

conspicuously consult the omniscient machine, regardless of existing climatic conditions. This timely ritual provides all viewers with regularly scheduled opportunities to eye-witness the wondrous weather-radar in action, as it perceives precipitation, stalks storms, gazes at ground clutter or relaxes in the off-mode.

Contrary to our expectations, though, occasionally radar is deceived. Instead of singling out legitimate patches of precipitation, as promised, sometimes radar is bamboozled into detecting flocks of birds, swarms of insects, and believe it or not, *angels!* If these false echoes were easy to discern from true weather, I would steadfastly uphold the honor of weather-radar. However, a bird "blip" and a rain "blip" are indistinguishable to even the experienced radar technician, hence, we can never *really* be sure of exactly what it is that we're watching on weather-radar. With this in mind, it is conceivable that the "spotty light rainshowers" mentioned in a forecast could turn out to be "widely scattered starlings" *if* the prediction was based solely on radar information.

The problem of birds "fowling"-up weather radar is common. So common, in fact, that a special group of researchers conducted a study to determine the possible correlations between particular species and radar echoes. The chart below was compiled from their findings:

If radar echoes are:	**What to forecast (1)**	**or**	**(2)**
intense and fast paced	heavy rain, strong winds and vivid lightning		shore birds
dim and sluggish	steady light rain		sea gulls
diffused and sporadic in their appearance	intermittent rainshowers, intermittent snowshowers		migrating songbirds

Not being an ornithologist, I personally prefer the

curious, spurious radar-returns known as *angels*. Synonymized with the scientific term *anomalous propagation*, according to the *Glossary of Meteorological Terms*, an *angel* is a physical phenomenon NOT visible to the unaided eye. In other words, angels are hallucinations of the "infallible" radarscope.

Sometimes, but definitely NOT always, angels appear simultaneously with temperature inversions. Distorted by the abnormal vertical temperature arrangement, the radio-waves discharged from the radar transmitter become confused, and return fraudulent data to the set-receiver. In turn, the radarscreen exhibits coherent *rain* echoes, despite the fact skies may be crystal clear for miles around! (When normal atmospheric conditions exist, the inversion excuse is invalid, so numerous angel sightings remain unexplained.)

There is no etymological record of the radar word *angel*. Therefore, we are tempted to guess why that particular word *angel* was chosen to describe the phantom images detected by radar. Are radar angels more mysterious than we think?

Are Radar's Angels *Really* Angels?

The naked eye was put to shame,
An eon after Eden,
Now we dare not nudely look
At things we did back then.

It used to be we'd look for rain,
Outside we read the skies.
But now unless some scope you use,
You've nothing seen but lies.

There are telescopes and microscopes,
And periscopes galore.
Binoculars and mini-scopes.
(To spy on folks next door!)

Radar is the special eye,
That weathermen look through,
Gazing at the cluttered ground
Whenever the skies are blue.

Helpful? Yes. Sometimes it is,
Yet often it's a pain;
Detecting things like bugs and birds,
Instead of storms and rain.

And what commotion it can cause
(That mighty radar screen);
When nothing's there, but still it sees,
The "things" that are unseen.

Angels someone named them and,
I like to think it's true.
Radar does detect the cherubs
Guarding me and you. *

Noah's Arc . . .

Rainbow Roy says, "Don't forget,
If it's sunny while it's wet,
Find a rainbow, count each hue;
Red, orange, yellow, green and blue,

Indigo and violet." (WOW)
It represents an age-old vow:
Despite the fact it rained and poured,
A promise to us from the Lord,
Said never would another Flood
Drown the world and leave just mud. *

In this chapter, I'd like you to become acquainted with a good buddy of mine whom I met several years ago in the United States Navy. His name: Roy G. Biv. Nicknamed "Rainbow Roy," Roy helped the rest of us swabbies remember the color sequence in nature's most cherished light display: the rainbow. While the remainder of our company guarded laundry bags and peeled potatoes,

Roy was singled out for this special duty because each letter in his name conveniently coincided with one of the seven colors of the rainbow; **r**ed, **o**range, **y**ellow, **g**reen, **b**lue, **i**ndigo, **v**iolet.

Unfairly defined in most meteorological manuals as a "luminous meteor consisting of concentric colored bands," a rainbow rightly deserves to be associated with adjectives like gorgeous, awesome, mystical, elusive, and above all, *heavenly*. *Everything* about a rainbow suggests that it *is* "other-worldly." A rainbow begins and ends somewhere which, in reality, is nowhere. A rainbow will shyly and silently retreat from one's advance: however, it shadows in pursuit an observer that dares to walk away from its splendor. Unpredicted, it appears suddenly, lingers mere moments, then fades without adieus, leaving no visible tracks or trails, except in the minds of those lucky enough to view it.

The ancient Japanese recognized the rainbow as a "floating bridge of heaven." The Norsemen knew it as the "bridge of gods." Many American Indian tribes considered it the "pathway of souls." Personally, I prefer calling it NOAH'S ARC.

Following the Great Flood (Genesis 6-9), God spoke to Noah:

> *I solemnly promise you and your children and the animals you brought with you — all these birds and cattle and wild animals — that I will never again send another flood to destroy the earth. And I seal this promise with this sign: I have placed my rainbow in the clouds as a sign of my promise until the end of time, to you and all the earth. When I send clouds over the earth, the rainbow will be seen in the clouds, and I will remember my promise to you and to every being, that never again will the floods come and destroy all life. For I will see the rainbow in the clouds*

and remember my eternal promise to every living being on the earth. (Genesis 9:9-17)

In this passage, the Lord gives dual reasons for his display of the arc: to remind humans and to remind himself of the eternal promise. God's admittance in needing a visible reminder should be added assurance to all humans that we indeed are created in His likeness.

It is this Genesis connotation that we most frequently prescribe to the rainbow. However, the rainbow also has a very prominent symbolism when it's again presented in the Bible, in Revelation 4:3. In the final biblical book, John the Apostle envisions a rainbow encircling the heaven-based throne of the almighty King of kings. Almost like a coat-of-arms, a rainbow "glowing like an emerald" is exhibited over God's royal seat. Still an emblem of perpetual promise, Revelation's rainbow represents God's guarantee of Judgment Day.

Thousands of years later, to active Christians, the sight of a rainbow still sends chills down the spine, reminiscent of God's omnipresence, omnipotence, omniscience, and omni-beneficence. Furthermore, the rainbow denotes good fortune, assurance and favorable expectation.

It is interesting to note here that, despite its virtuous Christian implications, in many religions the rainbow is not associated with godliness, goodness, and glamour. On the contrary, people of certain countries dread the sight of a rainbow, considering it an evil omen, a sure sign of pending disaster. For instance, in Malaya, a conspicuous rainbow is a premonition that a prince's death will occur in the near future. In Romania, anyone passing beneath the rainbow arcs receives a most peculiar curse: they undergo an immediate sex change! And, throughout Europe, folks put the taboo on pointing at rainbows, believing one's finger will swell up and fall off if it's guilty of aiming at the multi-colored sky curves.

Another rather unique difference concerning the world-wide rainbow beliefs, where the rainbow is not viewed as some sort of bridge, it's often recognized as a supernatural sky serpent descending from the clouds to drink water (most prevalent among the Australian Aborigines, the Kumana of eastern Bolivia, and other South American Indian tribes).

The legend that some sort of valuable treasure can be found at the "end of the rainbow" is universally popular. This belief prompted the phrase "rainbow chaser," which refers to the ambitious, optimistic-type person attempting the impossible. In Silesia (a region of central Europe) rainbow chasers are never women. Why? Because in that land, they presume the pot of gold is deposited by angels and can *only* be discovered by a nude male.

Rene Descartes, famed French mathematician, is honored as the first person to accurately describe the *mechanics* of a rainbow.[1] Since Descartes' original explanation back in the early 1600's, scores and scores of other professionals have:

Analyzed and theorized
The colored arcs we see in skies;
Drawing graphs, preparing charts,
. . . criticizing all the parts.
Making fancy illustrations
(mocking our imaginations),
Their optic laws and frequencies
Condemn our treasured legacies.
They tell us "there's no need for guessing"
. . . but WHO'S the judge of what's a blessing. *

Does anyone have the right to destroy the magic and mystery of civilization's most beloved natural "wonder"? I definitely think not and, therefore, will make no attempt

1. Descartes was also first to describe the six-sided shape of snowflakes.

to lessen the rainbow's magnificence. I offer the following meteorological summaries only in sincere hopes that you, the reader, will gain a greater appreciation of God's creative genius.

A rainbow appears when sunlight passes through a veil of falling rain. Sunlight alone is white light, or as scientists say, *colorless*. However, *colorless* is a sure misnomer since squeezed inside of what we call *colorless* white light is the entire mass, mumbo-jumbo of all the spectral colors. Not until the sort of *blah* white light passes through the raindrops, though, do those colors escape. This happens since the raindrops are serving as tiny, liquid prisms, bending (refracting) the sunlight, and causing the white light (sunlight) to fan out into its beautiful spectrum of colors.

As we mentioned earlier in this chapter, the color sequence of a rainbow is red, orange, yellow, green, blue, indigo, and violet. This succession of colors is reliably constant, *if* only one rainbow exists. A singular rainbow is more properly titled a *primary* rainbow. On occasion, a second, much fainter rainbow appears, outside of the more prominent, primary bow. In the case of a *secondary* bow, two reflections are taking place within each raindrop. Because of the dual reflection, the order of colors in the secondary bow is reversed: violet, indigo, blue, green, yellow, orange and red.

Here are a couple of "tips" you might want to keep in mind, if you wish to improve your chances of seeing a rainbow:

1. Rainbows form opposite the sun's position in the sky.
2. Rainbows are most often discernible following "heat" thunderstorms of summer.

Rainbows form opposite the sun's position in the sky. Considering this bit of information, one should reason that in the hours before noon, it's the western skyline that will be the backdrop of any rainbows, since the sun rises in the east. Likewise, afternoon rainbows are displayed in the eastern sky as the sun slowly makes its journey to the western horizon.

Rainbows are most often discernible following the "heat" thunderstorms of summer. This advice will save you a lot of unnecessary frustration waiting for a rainbow *every* time it rains. When the weathercasters are preaching prolonged periods of precipitation associated with any kind of frontal systems, the formation of rainbows is quite unlikely. Extensive cloud layers usually succeed fronts once the rain ends. However, localized "heat" (convective) thunderstorms that are characteristic of summer are typified by abrupt clearing and immediate sunlight following devastating "dam-buster" rains.

For centuries, shepherds, farmers, and sailors have regarded rainbows as not only transient "treats" for the eyeball, but also as an invaluable forecasting aid. Once *you* become familiar with where and when to look for rainbows, you too might want to try your luck at forecasting, using the sky-arcs as the basis of your prognosis. Infinite oodles of rainbow weather-wisdoms exist in folklore that can add some "fizz and fun" to your first forecast. A partial list of these sayings is found on pages 141 and 142.

Let's examine one of the more popular jingles:
"Rainbow in the morning, sailor take warning
Rainbow in the night, sailor's delight."

First off, one basic concept of United States weather must be reviewed: Here in the Northern Hemisphere, weather systems travel from west to east (discovered by Ben Franklin, 1743). Now, we'll evaluate the folklore saying, step by step:

Step 1: Think . . . if there is a rainbow in the morning it must be in the western sky. Why? A rainbow forms opposite the sun, and before noon, the sun is rising in the east.

Step 2: THINK . . . if the sun is in the east, the rain-cloud and rainbow are in west.

Step 3: SAILOR TAKE WARNING . . . Weather in the west is traveling this way, bringing the rain in that cloud.

Step 4: THINK . . . A rainbow at night (which is really evening) is in the eastern sky. Why? A rainbow forms opposite the sun, and the evening sun is setting in the west.

Step 5: THINK . . . If the rainbow and its related raincloud are in the eastern sky, bad weather must already have passed our area.

Step 6: SAILOR'S DELIGHT? Yes, since weather travels from west to east.

Another folklore forecasting freebie is available from the rainbow, this one concerning its colors. Even though the color sequence of rainbows is constantly consistent, the intensities of the shades varies. Note the most dominant color in the observed bow, and check the chart below.

GREEN ► rain
RED ► rain and wind together
BLUE ► fair soon

The color code predictions are, for the most part, still a matter of speculation. Some meteorologists claim the intensity of certain shades is related to particulants in the atmosphere, such as algae, pollen, volcanic dust, or forest fire smoke, etc.

To the majority of the populous, primary and secondary rainbows are deemed commonplace and rather unmysterious. However, many extraordinary bows have been reported that seem scientifically unfounded, defying known optic laws of reflection, refraction and what not. Many of these rather "rare" rainbows are recorded in William R. Corliss' *Handbook*

Of Unusual Natural Phenomena, such as intersection rainbows, inverted rainbows, fog bows, and lunar rainbows. One report even relates the simultaneous sighting of SIX rainbows by one observer. It is these strange sightings that strengthen the likelihood of the "godliness" of ALL rainbows.

Also, tending to favor the divine aspect of rainbows is the number of colors displayed in its spectrum: SEVEN. No one (as far as I know) has ever scientifically discovered why a "rainbow of colors" refers to a certain seven colors. However, the sacredness of the number seven is traceable back to Genesis 1: "God blessed the seventh day." It was on day number seven God chose to relax following his stupendous task of Creation, and also it was on a number seven day that he chose to rest following the great Flood episode.

The holiness of the number seven endures throughout the Bible, but particularly in the account of the Deluge. Noah was pre-warned of the Flood's imminence seven days before the first drops fell. The raven and dove were released at seven-day intervals. And Noah and his family left the Ark to offer sacrifices on a seventh day.

Whether God originally intended the number of colors in a rainbow to be of some spiritual significance is not revealed to us in the Scriptures. However, the frequency in which seven appears in the Holy Book is too often to be considered "coincidental." Seven is a holy number. The rainbow is God's holy sign. Perhaps there is some unknown connection between the *seven* parts of the Lord's prayer, the *seven* archangels, the *seven* trumpets, the *seven* last words of Christ, the *seven* pillars of Wisdom, the *seven* braided locks of Samson, . . . etc., AND the *seven* colors of the rainbow. Will we ever know for sure?

Nevertheless, let us continue to religiously respect and revere the rainbow as appropriately as our Christian ancestors. The ephemeral glory of a rainbow is recreated and preserved in the very finest of sanctuaries throughout the world, in the form of ornately decorated arcs and archways and multi-colored stained glass windows.

Orbiting space ships to Saturn and Mars
Reveal the secrets of planets and stars.
They travel a distance we can't comprehend
(It's strange none have reached yet the place rainbows end.).

Another thing missing (to me it seems odd),
Inter-space journeys find no signs of God.
Despite all the miles, no "angels on high"
Have yet been reported by "the friendly skies."

Where is then the throne of the Savior, our Lord?
Is it somewhere the rockets and jets have all soared?
Or is it just hidden right under our nose?
Found by the faithful but "lost" to his foes.

Look closely and follow those colors, all seven;
A rainbow's arc bridges our world with God's heaven.
And if you search simply with pure heart and prayer
The rain and dark clouds of your life will turn fair. *

Rainbow Sayings:

"If there be a rainbow in the eve,
It will rain and leave.
But if there be a rainbow in the morrow,
It will neither lend nor borrow."

(Norsemen)

"Rainbow to the windward, foul falls the day,
Rainbow to the leeward, damp runs away."

"Dog in the morning, sailor take warning
Dog in the night, sailor's delight."

(sailors)

"Rainbows in the west bring light showers
Rainbows in the east promise good hunting."

(Indians)

The rainbow in the morning
Is the shepherd's warning
To carry his coat on his back.
The rainbow at night
Is the shepherd's delight.
For then no coat will be lack.

(*Weather Lore* Inwards)

"A rainbow at morn,
Put your hook in the corn.
A rainbow at eve,
Put your head in the sheave."

(farmers)

"Rainbow in the eastern sky,
The morrow will be dry.
Rainbow in the west that gleams,
Rain falls in the streams."

(Chinese)

"A weather gall at morn,
Fine weather all gone;
A rainbow towards night,
Fair weather in sight."

(Sailors)

"Rainbow in the east,
Sailors at peace.
Rainbow in the west,
Sailors in distress."

(Sailors)

O Holy Light!

Ring around the collar
For housewives is a pain.
But ring around the sun or moon
Helps us to forecast rain.

Sometimes colored, sometimes white,
Halos, indeed, are odd.
What science can't explain for us
We understand thru God. *

A halo is a circular display of light *sometimes* surrounding the sun or moon. *Sometimes* halos appear white, *sometimes* halos appear as a circle of colors, and *sometimes* halos don't appear at all!!!

What causes halos?

White halos are caused by light *reflection* off the tiny ice crystals that make up very high clouds known as cirrostratus, usually.

Colored halos are products of light *refraction* through

the cirrostratus ice crystals, usually. The color arrangement is the same order, but a reversal of the hue assortment displayed in a rainbow: red, orange, yellow, green, blue, indigo, violet (red being closest to the light source).

Reported an average of two hundred days a year, the most common halo possesses a radius of twenty-two degrees, resulting from refraction through hexagonal prisms (as in ice crystals) at a sixty degree angle.

Several other sizes and types of halos are theoretically explained, too. (see page 146) However, there are hundreds and thousands of halo sightings reported that cannot be understood since they ignore and/or defy the usual laws of optics. A plethora of these incidents are recorded in the *Handbook of Unusual Phenomena*, compiled by William R. Corliss, including double halos, offset halos, multiple halos, multiple-complex halos, intersecting halos, and halos with no apparent origin.

The mysterious accounts of halos, along with the numerous *sometime's*, *if's* and *maybe's* that are interspersed in their scientific explanations, allow and seemingly encourage our spiritual beliefs and imaginations to run wild. Personally, I've been catering to an uncanny curiosity and fascination for halos over the past dozen years, and I've read numerous textbook explanations of:

HOW they get there
WHAT they do.
WHY you see 'em,
WHAT you view,
The angles and
the radii,
The saturation
of the sky,
The prism spectrum,

light diffused,
And after "all" I'm
still confused.
Some are different,
quite unique,
Elliptical,
but not oblique,
The rules oft change
so as to please us,
But science stuff
Doesn't mention Jesus,
And maybe we
Will never know,
What made God's Son's
halo glow;
But when you view
the sun or moon;
That HALO is a sign
that soon,
Rain will come
with life refreshed,
Showers of blessing,
God has blessed. *

Yes, despite my knowledge of the vast and complicated meteorological "how's and why's" of halos, I still prefer to view the luminous ring as a sign from Above: a heavenly omen that rain will come, a secondary reminder of the never-ending promise God made to Noah, and an overall assurance of the Lord's omnipresence.

It is interesting to note that there are two other terms used interchangeably with the word *halo;* glory and nimbus. In meteorology, *glory* is used synonymously with *halo*, yet glory is a word generally meaning *heaven*. In theology, *nimbus* is a word occasionally used synonymously with *halo*, but *nimbus* is an every-day weather word recognized in the *International Cloud Atlas* as a low, dark cloud that brings precipitation. A *coincidental* cross-reference? . . . Who knows?

And what about Cellini's halo: a diffuse white ring surrounding the head portion of a shadow on a lawn covered with morning dew? This particular type of halo is named after Benvenuto Cellini, the man who first clearly discussed the peculiar phenomena.

As with all halos, *sometime's, if's* and *maybe's* abound in the professional explanations that attempt to accurately define Cellini's halo *(heligenschein)*. It forms, *sometimes,* when dew is present on a grassy surface *if* the solar elevation is low, allowing a great distance from the shadow to the observer. It is produced by external reflection on the surface of tiny water droplets, *possibly* combined with diffraction effects. To the observer, it appears as if a holy light surrounds the shadow of one's own head; however, the halo is not visible to anyone else (Benvenuto Cellini regarded this halo as a divine sign of his own godliness).

The American Meteorological Society's *Glossary of Meteorological* terms states: "Some halos theoretically predicted have not yet been reported; some that have been reported have not yet been explained." The halo encircling the head of Christ is just one of the many halos with a missing explanation. Through hearsay evidence and great works of ancient art, we believe Christ's halo glowed continuously, even at night, . . . but a reflection *cannot* occur in the darkness. This argument is repeatedly used to discount the probability of Jesus' halo. However, the age-old mystery is simply solved through faith, for Jesus told us, "I am the light of the world." (John 8:12)

Halo Lore

"If the moon shows a silver shield

Don't be afraid to reap your field.
But if she rises haloed round
Soon you'll walk on flooded ground."

"The moon with a circle
brings water in her beak.
The circle of the sun
wets the shepherd."

"When the sun is in his house
it will rain soon." (Indian)

"Last night the moon had a golden ring,
Tonight there is no moon." (sailor)

"When the sun retires to his house (halo),
it is because it is going to rain outside."

"Last night the sun went pale to bed,
The moon in halos hid his head."

"When the moon wears a halo
Around her head she will cry
Before morning and her tears
will reach you before tomorrow."

Over the years, halos have built themselves an enormous reputation as an accurate rain sign. All these adages, generations old, are delivering the message that halos are formed if high ice crystal clouds (cirrostratus) are present. It is cirrostratus clouds that are the first forerunners of major weather systems that generally bring precipitation. The time element involved depends on the speed of the approaching weather front. On the average, cold fronts travel at about 20 to 30 mph, and warm fronts advance somewhat slower at 15 mph or less.

Halos appear to grow and move away as the weather

system moves it closer to the ice crystals, and the clouds overhead become lower.

"The bigger the ring, the nearer the wet."

"When the wheel is far, the storm is n'ar,
When the wheel is n'ar, the storm is far."

Some old-timers firmly believe that the stars visible within the halo ring denote how many days of rain are in the forecast. Also, if more than five stars appear, colder weather will follow. Fewer than five stars indicates warmer weather.

Ocean Commotion

Cyclones, serpents, Satan,
Devils in disguise,
Evil forces all awhirl,
Striking by surprise.

Death, destruction, poison, pain,
Raisin' "holy hell,"
Beelzebub's beneath the deep
And casts each stormy spell. *

To the untrained eye, a weather map resembles a piece of string-art produced by a preschooler. Strange squiggles swirl here and there like so many worms tossed into a bait pail, worms gone wild.

Actually, though, the squiggles possess a very sophisticated title: *isobars* (*iso* meaning equal and *bar* meaning weight). Isobars connect points of equal air pressure on the earth's surface, and despite their apparent disorder, each set neatly conforms around a center point of either high or low barometer readings. Around the zones of maximum barometric pressure, the wind flows clockwise, or anti-cyclonic; however, the low pressure areas are distinguished by their counter-clockwise airflow, professionally deemed *cyclonic*.

In researching the etymology (word origin) of *cyclone*, I was dumbfounded to learn how near-to-correct my silly "worms-gone-wild" concept had been. Cyclone is of Greek ancestry, originally meaning *coils of a snake*.

Continuing to read, I found some interesting analogies concerning nature's fiercest and feared storms. Each idea seemed like unto a random jigsaw piece, anxious to be annexed with its sister puzzle parts. Because of their incongruity, each fascinating fragment will be presented individually for your review.

The first puzzle piece to examine pertains to the question: Why are hurricanes spawned in the Bermuda Triangle?

Briefly stated, the Bermuda Triangle is a three-sided stretch of the lower Atlantic Ocean, noted throughout history for its rash of unexplained disasters, including the loss of thousands of lives. Strangely enough, the triangle region corresponds almost precisely with the ocean expanse statistically famed for tropical cyclones, which develop over waters heated to temperatures above eighty degrees Fahrenheit.

Scanning through the forty-first chapter of Job, mention is made of Leviathan, a sea serpent that "makes the depths boil like a pot." (Job 41:31) And, just where are the depths? The deepest "depths" are the Puerto Rican Trench at the bottom of the Bermuda Triangle (bottoming out at 27,500 feet) and the Mariana Trench near the Devil's Sea off the Japanese coast (36,198 feet).

What's most significant about the Devil's Sea? The Devil's Sea parallels the Bermuda Triangle in its reputation for misfortune. Likewise, the most terrible tropical cyclones of the Eastern Hemisphere form in its waters. Are these two depths "the gates of deep darkness" into the underworld? (Job 38:16-17)

What is the name given to tropical cyclones in the Eastern Hemisphere? *Typhoon* is the name applied to storms of hurricane strength in the Eastern Hemisphere. It is a word derived from the Greek/Roman mythological sea monster, *Typhon*, which possessed many heads and breathed fire, a creature with nearly the same written resemblance as Leviathan, "a swiftly moving serpent, the coiling, writhing serpent." (Isaiah 27:1) The key words in the Isaiahic description are *coiling* and *serpent.* Check back and notice the meaning of the word *cyclone:* coils of a snake!

Could Leviathan and the seven-headed creature of Revelation be related? The seven-headed creature envisioned thrice by John in Revelation is symbolic of the devil, as is Leviathan in the Old Testament. Like Leviathan, the Revelation monster is an evil beast seen "rising up out of the sea." (Revelation 13:1) Another coincidence, *hurricane* is a word derived from *huracan,* signifying "evil spirit" in the language of the Carribean Indians.

Let's return, now to the original question posed on the puzzle piece: Why are hurricanes spawned in the Bermuda Triangle? Some claim the vicious storms could be "caused by spiritual contacts between God and Satan at the 'gates of Hell' in the continuing battle between good and evil." (George Johnson and Don Tanner) *The Bible and the Bermuda Triangle)*

Granted, this theory is deemed idiotic by meteorologists and climatologists. However, their more verbose explanations are usually so pierced with perplexing pits that the theories are rarely received with widespread credibility. The public is left primed for more supportive evidence, presented in layperson's language.

Actually, the more honest author will openly admit "there is still no exact understanding of the triggering mechanisms involved in hurricane generation." (James Ruffner and Frank Bair: *The Weather Almanac)* This confession is accepted. We realize study of the Triangle is difficult. According to the assistant professor of physics at Longwood College in Farmville, Virginia, there is some force that causes even satellite photos to "black out" the Bermuda Triangle region. Scores of passes, relayed back to earth via four NOAA weather satellites, have proven space-age technology to be incapable of filming the mysterious Triangle sea segment. But, research of the deep continues. This in itself is another oddity! The Old Testament term often used interchangeably with "deep" is *sheol*, a word meaning "a place of inquiry."

Is it possible that the Devil, who appeared to Eve as a "serpent," fell from heaven (Luke 10:18) and was cast into the deep we refer to as the Bermuda Triangle? The notion is not new. It has been in existence for centuries. In fact, only recently has the name *Bermuda* Triangle been ascribed to the terrible ocean tract. Previously it was simply regarded: the *Devil's* Triangle.

Another antiquated anecdote to review as we attempt to solve our puzzle involves the *horse latitudes*. What are the *horse latitudes?*

Horse latitudes is a popular nickname for the doldrums, the ocean areas characterized by winds of little strength and extremely high barometric pressure (charted at 30°N and 30°S, latitude). The title is derived from the Spanish expression *Golfo de Las Yeguas,* or "mares gulf." However, the *reason* for this strange surname is usually listed as "obscure." There are, of course, theories that account for the unusual designation, based on some interesting deductions.

1. Before meeting its mysterious fate, Atlantis was famed for its abundance of horses. It is said that on the legendary continent, horses were first domesticated and bred for sport racing. When the land disappeared, sailors repeatedly encountered hundreds of dead horses floating on the water surface in the doldrums region, hence, the name *Horse latitude*.
2. A few histologists pin-point the Bermuda Triangle as the ocean expanse under which Atlantis lies hidden. This hypothesis, which for years was unbased, has recently been bolstered by a series of remarkable discoveries. In 1968-70, a Yale

zoology professor reported detecting an ancient shipping center submerged beneath the deep waters off the Florida coast. Dr. Valentine is convinced his find points to Atlantis. Also, validating the legend of Atlantis is the "Bimini Road" discovery of 1975. According to the *Daily Breeze* newspaper (May 24, 1975), members of the International Explorers Society eye-witnessed an underwater road of rock estimated to be over 6,000 years old. The location: the Bermuda Triangle, immediately off the coast of the Bahamas.

3. Since the myth of Poseidon and the legends of Lucifer parallel in many instances, some specialists suggest they could be the same person. This curious concept sheds light on a yet untouched assemblage of biblical verses listed in Revelation concerning the Armageddon war in which two hundred million horses actively participate. Some believe the horses now confined to "the deep" will be released to take part in God's final judgment battle.

Consider the unexplained development of tropical cyclones. Impossible to forecast, some tropical disturbances fizzle out. But, on the other hand, other storms of identical character mature into one of nature's most savage storms, releasing energy amounts equal to five hundred thousand A-bombs in twenty-four hours.

Also, ask yourself the question: Are scientists *unwilling* (as they say) to tame hurricanes because the storms aid in preserving global heat stability or are they secretly fearful of angering the demons that just might be the unexplained driving force behind the terrible tempests?

HAZEL, CONNIE, AUDREY, CAROL,
and a hundred more —
Formed out in the oceans calm,
Then waged a mighty war.

Weaponed with strong winds and rain
(clever strategy)
Snaking "long erratic paths,"
Nurtured by the sea.

Rattling every tree around,
Signaling its advance.
Its venom science can't combat,
Or charm into a trance.

Its eye is "open" from its birth,
But what's it looking for?
A key to fit the gates of hell,
Or some unlocked back door?

Devouring prey in one huge gulp
(A habit very queer).
Some folks in surge tides, sudden struck,
Forever disappear!

Perhaps someday we'll know just why
The evil forces brew . . .
Are cyclones just another way
*The devil gets his due?**

Drought, Dust, Devils and Dog Days

Dry up and blow away, you creep,
This drought has done me in.
If Coppertone could see me now,
They'd love my brick-red skin.

Dry-rot has plighted trees and crops,
Like no one's seen in years —
A drought so dry that even babes,
Are dry behind the ears.

"Dry-eyed" I face the saddest news,
'Cause tears require water,
And though I laugh at humor — dry
I really hadn't ought'er.

"Dry runs?" — We practice everyday,
So we're prepared for rain.
(Dry-cleaning socks and underwear,
I find a royal pain.)

This bone-dry spell is all our fault
(You must think I'm "all wet").
Just pray to God to end the drought,
And rain is what we'll get. *

Why are the *worst* days of summer named after "man's *best* friend?" (The man accredited with the first usage of the expression "a dog is man's best friend" was Senator George C. Vast, Warrensburg, Missouri, 1876.)

This question, or one quite like it, befuddles the minds of millions year after year. Many persons believe the title is associated with supposed epidemic levels of rabies during the fervid months. However, veterinarians report that in a normal year more rabid cases are reported in spring and autumn than during the dog days. In an attempt to "teach an old dog new tricks," the dogmas of dog days will hereafter be discussed.

First off, the cuddly, cordial, canine creature we now cherish as a household pet has *not* always been so beloved. For eons, the dog was considered a blatant beast, guilty of the most filthy, disgusting habits. Only in the more recent centuries have dogs undergone a reputation-reversal.

Throughout the Scriptures, *dog* is used as a degrading expression. Isaiah makes mention of "dumb dogs" and "greedy dogs," (Isaiah 56:10, 11 KJV) and King Solomon proverbially states "as a dog returns to his vomit, so a fool repeats his folly." (Proverbs 26:11) It is from this well-established biblical implication that a number of contemporary *dog* phrases have derived, including "gone to the dogs," "you dirty dog," "throw it to the dogs," and "call off the dogs." Undoubtedly, the same attitude of ardent abhorrence enforced the tenor of the term now in question: dog days. But, the dog days are referred to as dog days even in areas where it does not pertain to contemptuous weather. Why? Keep reading . . .

The dog days aren't just any random group of hot and sticky summer days. The dog days are a specific forty days of midsummer, commencing the third of July and terminating the eleventh of August. This particular timespan represents the period during which a certain star, Sirius, rises and sets at approximately the same time as the sun.

Alone, Sirius is a star of extreme importance. It holds the distinction of being the most luminous star in our heavens, estimated to be twice as brilliant as the sun and three hundred times brighter than the faintest visible stars. Sirius also is noted for belonging to a family of fourteen stars that compose one of our principal constellations: Canis Major. (see below) The member stars of the Canis Major cluster form an imaginary sky arrangement that takes the shape of a large "pooch." It is from this apparent pattern that the constellation received its name: Canis Major, meaning "Big Dog" (Latin). Because of Sirius' dominance in the Big Dog group, it sports the "pet" name of the Dog Star.

Sirius the Dog Star
Constellation: Canis Major

While the Dog Star is busy playing follow-the-leader with Ole' Sol each summer, another significant event is in simultaneous occurrence: Thermometers are climbing to their annual high points. Searching for a logical explanation for this oddity, the ancients hit upon the idea that the earth must be receiving a double dosage of heat during the Dog Days. One portion of the heat was known to come from the sun. The excess degrees were presumed to be a contribution of the Dog Star, Sirius, a name originating from the Greek adjective *seirios*, meaning "hot and scorching."

In Egypt, the yearly reappearance of Sirius in the morning sky was a celebrated sight. It heralded the rising of the Nile's flood-waters, after which the season of agricultural activity began. On the other hand, though, away from the Nile, the Dog Star was regarded as a precursor of evil.

Whether Sirius is responsible for any of summer's infernal heat is still a debatable topic between opposing teams of "weather-ologists." Climatology experts deny the feasibility of such an antiquated notion, whereas astro-meteorologists convincingly uphold the theory that our planet is, and always has been, influenced by a multitude of cosmic what-nots, including stars, asteroids, meteorites, and comets. Nevertheless, the fact remains that yearly maximum temperatures are usually reached during the Dog Day period, with forty of our forty-eight contiguous states claiming all-time record highs during the legendary Dog Days. (see chart page 159)

Just as predictable as the return of summer's heat is the resurgence of the renowned, but vague, expression "it's hotter than hell." Depending on the geographical location one accepts as the homesite of Hell, the temperature implied in the trite saying can range anywhere from 100°F to 10,000°F! To some, Hades is situated in the core of the earth where daily temperatures average a sizzling 10,000 degrees. But, to folks residing in lower Michigan, Hell is but a mini-metropolis (population 54) northwest of Detroit where the hottest temperature EVER recorded was a modest 104° back on June 29, 1952. And, most extraordinary of all, Jewish cabalists (members of "cabala" which is "an occult

RECORD HIGHEST TEMPERATURES BY STATES

State and Temp.		Date	Station
Alabama	112	September 5, 1925	Centerville
Alaska	100	June 27, 1915	Fort Yukon
Arizona	127	July 7, 1905	Parker
Arkansas	120	August 10, 1936	Ozark
California	134	July 10, 1913	Greenland Ranch
Colorado	118	July 11, 1888	Bennett
Connecticut	105	July 22, 1926	Waterbury
Delaware	110	July 21, 1930	Millsboro
D.C.	106	July 20, 1930	Washington
Florida	109	June 29, 1931	Monticello
Georgia	112	July 24, 1952	Louisville
Hawaii	100	April 27, 1931	Pahala
Idaho	118	July 28, 1934	Orofino
Illinois	117	July 14, 1954	East St. Louis
Indiana	116	July 14, 1936	Collegeville
Iowa	118	July 20, 1934	Keokuk
Kansas	121	July 24, 1936	Alton (near)
Kentucky	114	July 28, 1930	Greensburg
Louisiana	114	August 10, 1936	Plain Dealing
Maine	105	July 10, 1911	North Bridgton
Maryland	109	July 10, 1935	Cumberland and Frederick
Massachusetts	106	July 4, 1911	Lawrence
Michigan	112	July 13, 1936	Mio
Minnesota	114	July 6, 1936	Moorhead
Mississippi	115	July 29, 1930	Holly Springs
Missouri	118	July 14, 1954	Warsaw and Union
Montana	117	July 5, 1937	Medicine Lake
Nebraska	118	July 24, 1936	Minden
Nevada	122	June 23, 1954	Overton
New Hampshire	106	July 4, 1911	Nashua
New Jersey	110	July 10, 1936	Runyon
New Mexico	116	July 14, 1934	Orogrande
New York	108	July 22, 1926	Troy
North Carolina	109	September 7, 1954	Weldon
North Dakota	121	July 6, 1936	Steele
Ohio	113	July 21, 1934	Gallipolis (near)
Oklahoma	120	July 26, 1943	Altus and Alva
Oregon	119	August 10, 1898	Pendleton
Pennsylvania	111	July 10, 1936	Phoenixville
Rhode Island	102	July 30, 1949	Greenville
South Carolina	111	June 28, 1954	Camden
South Dakota	120	July 5, 1936	Gannvalley
Tennessee	113	August 9, 1930	Perryville
Texas	120	August 12, 1936	Seymour
Utah	116	June 28, 1892	St. George
Vermont	105	July 4, 1911	Vernon
Virginia	110	July 15, 1954	Balcony Falls
Washington	118	August 5, 1961	Ice Harbor Dam
West Virginia	112	July 10, 1936	Martinsburg
Wisconsin	114	July 13, 1936	Wisconsin Dells
Wyoming	114	July 12, 1900	Basin

religious philosophy developed by certain Jewish rabbis, based on a mystical interpretation of the Scriptures." *Webster's New World Dictionary* ©1968) divided Hell into seven sub-levels, each being sixty times hotter than the preceding level.

Level 1:	Gehennom	. . . the heat 60 times that of fire
Level 2:	Gates of Death	60 times hotter than Gehennom
Level 3:	Shadow of Death	60 times hotter than the Gates of Death
Level 4:	Pit of Corruption	60 times hotter than Shadow of Death
Level 5:	Mire of Clay	60 times hotter than Pit of Corruption
Level 6:	Abaddon	60 times hotter than the Mire of Clay
Level 7:	Sheol	420 times hotter than fire

Hell, Michigan
(see page 158)

How many times have you been guilty of haphazardly comparing local weather with the climate of Hell? For your convenience in making such analogies more meteorologically accurate or perhaps, just for "the hell of it," below are some climatological statistics from Hell. (provided by the Chamber of Commerce, Hell, Michigan)

Month	Hell's Average Heat	Hell's Average Cold
January	28	—10
February	34	— 7
March	38	6
April	43	28
May	52	33
June	63	41
July	78	52
August	72	45
September	67	43
October	58	38
November	46	33
December	37	20

Average first frost (when Hell freezes over) — September 20.

Hotter than Hell? . . . 104°F record high: June 29, 1962.

Colder than Hell? . . . —31°F record low: January 26, 1978.

A probable spin-off from the "hotter than hell" concept is the link between dust and demons. As summer's hellish heat wrings the last drop of moisture out of the soil, the fine particles of dried ground are easily whisked aloft by invisible convection currents. Because no "apparent" adverse weather conditions motivate the dust, the supernatural is suspected, the unseen force is assigned to the Feverish Fiend: the Devil. Therefore, we find the following two terms listed in weather glossaries:

Dancing Devil: a rapidly spiraling column of air developing over droughty land (also known as "devil," "satan," "desert devil," and "sand devil").

Dust Devils: a well-developed dancing devil carrying significant amounts of dust into the air. Dust devils develop over areas where there is a steep lapse rate (the decrease of temperature with height.)

Dust is but a symptom of a more distressing disease: drought. Distinct from other meteorological "killers" (like hurricanes, lightning, and floods), drought is an insidious phenomena, characterized by its slow and silent destruction. Possible in any month of the year, drought develops during prolonged periods of below normal precipitation. The persistent lack of adequate moisture gradually leads to the dehydration of plant and animal life, and water levels in lakes and rivers become dangerously low.

Vigorous research programs are now under way, aimed at pinpointing the cause of drought. Volumes of high-tech explanations have already been printed, citing such things as "shifting ocean currents," "varying wind patterns," "sterile clouds," and "abnormal solar action." All of the hypotheses (though different in context) share the characteristic of being incomplete. In each case, the reader is left wondering, "What causes the 'causes' of drought?" The answer is found in the Bible.

Moses is speaking . . . Deuteronomy 28:15, 23, 24:

> *"If you won't listen to the Lord your God and won't obey these laws I am giving you today (The Commandments), then all these curses shall come upon you . . . The heavens above you will be as unyielding as bronze and the earth beneath will be as iron. The land will become as dry as dust for lack of rain, and dust storms shall destroy you."*

The answer scientists eagerly seek is obvious: God is the fundamental force which produces any intermediate causes of drought.

Droughts are not to be considered accidental. Granted, graphs and charts of drought cycles *do* form a "composite of bewildering confusion and little accuracy," but this mumble-jumble of information best serves to exemplify God's ultimate control over the condition. When and where God decides punishment by drought is necessary, drought occurs. Whether or not his decision harmonizes with human-prediction is irrelevant.

The Bible provides two specific instances in which God utilizes drought as a means of chastisement for disobedient earthlings. In 1 Kings 16-18, we read that a certain king named Ahab built a temple for worship to the pagan sun god, Baal. By promoting the heathen religion, Ahab "did more to anger the Lord God of Israel than any of the other Kings." (1 Kings 16:33) Consequently, because of the Lord's extreme displeasure in Israel's outright violation of his Commandments, he withheld all rain *and dew*, for three years. And, in Haggai 1:10, the Lord directly informs prophet Haggai that he is "holding back the rain from heaven and giving you (Israel) such scant crops." The reason? The lack of public concern over the rebuilding of the Temple. God's disgust with his people over their disinterest resulted in the following divine resolution: "I (God) have called for a drought upon the land, yes, and in the highlands, too: a drought to wither the grain and grapes, and olives and all your other crops, a drought to starve both you and all your cattle, and ruin everything you have worked so hard to get." (Haggai 1:11) (quote from *1001 Questions Answered About Earthquakes, Avalanches, Floods and Other Natural Disasters*, p. 248.)

Twentieth century technology has advanced to the point that the effects of drought can now be controlled, to some extent. Conservation and rationing of available water is being practiced, as well as redistribution of water surplus to areas of scarcity. Artificial rainmaking methods and desalination plants are also operative and effective on a small scale basis. But, despite people's ability to delay the inconveniences caused by drought, the drought itself, cannot be eliminated or prevented by human ingenuity or intervention.

Is there any way possible that we can escape the suffering induced by drought? Yes, and once again, the Bible holds the answer: ". . . if you will carefully obey all of his commandments . . . and if you will love the Lord your God with all your hearts and souls, and will worship him, then he will continue to send both the early and late rains that will produce wonderful crops of grain, grapes for your vine, and olive oil." (Deuteronomy 11:13, 14)

A favorable climate is available to any nation that reverently submits to God and his government. It sounds so simple. Yet, why is this important covenant ignored? Why do we, as citizens, complain about contrary climatic conditions and allow huge sums of federal dollars to be pumped into weather modification projects? If dependable, favorable weather is desired, we've been instructed how to get it; our money and humanpower would be better aimed at achieving a united God-oriented kingdom.

Sirius Business

"A baleful sign, for it brings to mortals much fiery heat." Homer

"Sirius parches head and knees and the skin is dry though heat." Eighth century B.C., Hesoid

"When Sirius parches head and knees and the body is dried-up by reason of the heat, then sit in the shade and drink." Hesoid

"The Dog Star, that burning constellation, when he brings drought and disease on sickly mortals, rises and saddens the sky with inauspicious light." Virgil

Our Prodigal Sun

Sunrise, sunset, solar flare;
Who hung the sun away out there?
Suntan, Sunkist, solar cell;
Fire, Furnace; hot as Hell
Sunspot, sunlight, tall sunflower,
Who created solar power?
Men with brains all think they know,
Out of nowhere it did grow . . .
Suddenly, a giant "pop."
(When will all this nonsense stop?)
Turn to Chapter One, sixteen,
Simple story, short and clean,
It was on day number four,
*God made the sun for "ever more."**

"Then God said, 'Let there be bright lights in the sky to give light to the earth and to identify the day and the night; they shall bring about the seasons on the earth, and mark the days and years. And so it was. For God made two huge

lights, the sun and moon, to shine down upon the earth — the larger, the sun, to preside over the day . . ." (Genesis 1:14-16)

The sun is an invention of God. No other powerplant is worthy of its comparison. The sun is a complete, complex generating system with a near-to-continuous energy output "guestimated" to be equivalent to *230 trillion* horsepower. Indeed, it is a prodigal sun. Each second it dispels into space more energy than earthlings have consumed since time began. Of all its excessive power emissions, though, only a mere fraction is directed toward our "chosen" planet. Precisely calculated, so as not to disrupt the equilibrium necessary to support life, God permits only two billionths worth of sun's radiation to penetrate the earth's atmosphere. However, that seemingly minor portion of force that *is* designed to seep through the earth's atmospheric strata is what triggers the world's weather and brings about the seasons.

The magnificence of the sun has been recognized for eons. Early gratification of its splendor was expressed in the development of numerous sun-worshiping religions. These solar cults were based on the belief that the sun *was* God, not a creation of God. Helios, Apollo, Ur — they all were sun-gods. In fact, excavations have proven that sun dieties reigned in all of the great civilizations of antiquity, including Egypt, Greece, Babylonia, China, and Peru.

Problems with competitive sun-worshiping religions were pressing and recurrent during the Old Testament era. In strict defiance of the Lord's Commandments, an indeterminate number of Israelites were lured into sun idolatry by Baalites. The Baalites revered the sun god Baal. (Baal is also biblically referenced as Bel, Baalim, and Belim: Jeremiah 32:29, Jeremiah 19:5, 2 Kings 23:12, Numbers 22:41, Numbers 25:3-18, Deuteronomy 4:16, 1 Kings 16:31-33, 2 Kings 10:22, Isaiah

46:1, Judges 2:11, Judges 10:10.) They offered to him sacrifices of human children, and performed acts of self-torture as part of their religious rites.

All of Israel's finest leaders — Moses, Joshua, Jeremiah, Elijah, and Isaiah — were confronted with situations concerning the heathen god, Baal. In Numbers 25:3, Moses reports that many of his young men were seduced by Baalites in Acacia, and "before long all Israel was joining freely in the worship of Baal, the god of Moab; and the anger of the Lord was hot against his people." Due to his fury, God commanded Moses "to execute all who had worshiped Baal" because the law specified "do not look up into the sky to worship the sun, moon or stars." (Deuteronomy 4:19)

The curse of the three-year drought (1 Kings 17 — see page 8) was resultant of God's disgust with Israel under the government of a Baal-worshiping king. Ahab "built a temple and an altar for Baal in Samaria" and "did more to anger the Lord God of Israel than any of the other kings of Israel before him." (1 Kings 16:32,33) It was during the same rainless period that Elijah challenged the prophets of Baal to prove *their* god's "supposed" authenticity. The agreement terms were as follows: "Pray to your god (Baal) and I will pray to the Lord and the god who answers by sending fire to light the wood is the true God." (1 Kings 18:24) Despite feverish supplication on behalf of the Baalites, the pagan god was deaf to their request. The Lord God of Israel, though, quickly responded to Elijah's prayer and all 450 prophets of Baal were slain that day at Mt. Carmel.

The cult of Sol Invictus rivaled and attempted to eliminate Christianity during the latter part of the third century. Diocletian, the ill-famed Roman Emperor, professed, practiced, and promoted the pagan religion of the "unconquered Sun" right through his sovereignty. To Christians wishing to escape his persecution, Sol Invictus was offered as the only "spiritual" alternative. Those persons refusing to transfer their faith to the heathen god were scheduled for mass martyrization at government-operated pits. (The pits were pre-stocked with hungry lions au gratis the malevolent Diocletian.) Sol Invictus continued to be a strong adversary of Christianity until Constantine's "soldiers of the Cross" finally defeated the fanatical followers of the Unconquered Sun at the battle of Milivia Bridge, A.D. 312.

One other solar sect that proved to be a serious threat to the early Christian church was Mithraism. Mithras, the pagan god of light and truth, was identified as the sun, and Mithraists were convinced that belief in their god insured immortality. A portion of the Mithraistic doctrine paralleled the teachings of Christ and served to confuse new Christian converts who were easily led astray. Only after years of struggle did Christianity triumph over the false religion of Mithras, but not before it had left its mark.

The most significant, long-lasting "after effect" of Mithraism concerns Christmas. Mithras was thought to be reborn annually on the winter solstice, a date marked on the calendars of that age as December 25. (The Julian calendar, introduced by Julius Caesar in 46 B.C., was in use during the Mithraistic period. Today, we use a Gregorian calendar which is a revised version of the older Julian calendar. Introduced by Pope Gregory XIII in 1582, the Gregorian calendar made provisions for leap years every fourth year, except century years. Century years are "leap years" only if divisible by 400.) In celebration of the occasion, heathens honored Mithras by kindling tapers. The ceremonial candle-lighting, though, also appealed to Christians, and soon it became a Christian tradition performed each December 25. When church officials finally decided to adopt a day for commemorating the birth of Christ, "the doctors of the Church perceived that the Christians had a leaning to this festival, they took counsel, and resolved that the true Nativity should be solemnized on that day." (From *Adonis,*

Attis, Osiris, by J. G. Frazer. — words of an ancient Syrian Christian.) Had it not been for the influence of Mithraism on Christianity, Christmas, today, would probably be designated as January 6, the date the Eastern Church "unofficially" observed as Christ's birthday prior to A. D. 350.

Organized veneration of sun gods gradually declined and eventually disappeared, but the sun itself remained an item of utmost importance in all religions. Ever prominent in the daily skies, humankind recognized and respected the conspicuous ball-of-fire as being a symbol of God's constancy. Any interference with the sun's normal appearance was thereby interpreted as a divine sign, causing panic and uncertainty among the masses. Such was the case with solar eclipses.

Though first explained around 600 B.C., solar eclipses continued to cause widespread terror through the nineteenth century. Occurring infrequently, the sudden, temporary disappearance of the sun was mystical and defiant of any simple reasoning. Complicated astronomical tables were necessary to prefigure the time and location of the next eclipse, and these were neither accessible nor understandable to commoners. Therefore, eclipses occurred unannounced up until the mid 1700s. Records show that delirium, often leading to suicide, reached peak levels immediately following these unexpected sky events.

To Christians, the solar eclipse was reminiscent of Calvary. According to Luke 23:44, 45a: "By now it was noon, and darkness fell across the whole land for three hours, until three o'clock. The light from the sun was gone . . ." This spectacular eclipse, happening simultaneously with Christ's crucifixion, had not been predicted by any of the trusted sky-watchers of the age and does not coincide with past ecliptical cycles. Its timely occurrence was a demonstration of God's willful manipulation of the heavenly bodies and was read as a portrayal of the life of Christ. Jesus, the Light of the World, (symbolized by the sun) was temporarily "snuffed-out" by evildoers in this world (symbolized by darkness). But the reappearance of the sun, following the eclipse, represented the resurrection: the unfailing Light returning as promised.

Besides the solar eclipse, another baffling abnormality in the outward aspect of the sun was the sunspot. Galileo Galilei released initial studies on the spottiness of the sun in the early 1600's. Previous to Galileo's research, the sun was esteemed as a primary example of God's perfection. The idea that small, dark blotches might blemish the sun's surface insinuated that God had goofed and produced a faulty "cheap" product. Church authorities became vehement. Galileo's sunspot hypothesis (along with many of his scientific discoveries) was condemned by the Western Church, and Galileo was tried by the Roman Inquisition which handed him a heavy charge: guilty of heresy. Now, nearly 350 years later, an appeal to the Church has been made to allow Galileo a retrial. (*Science News*, November 1, 1980, p. 271.) Whether or not Galileo is freed of the conviction is insignificant, he spent the last four years of his life blind because of his curiousity over sunspots.

We no longer question the mere existence of sunspots. They are defacto. Satellite photography and powerful telescopes have repeatedly proven their presence on the sun's surface. Unfortunately, the "whys" and "wherefores" of the ornery spots are not as easily documented. Frankly, almost all information on sunspots is speculation. It is generally accepted that the blotches are cooler than the remainder of the solar exterior, and they are probably resultant of the sun's uneven rotation. Only the repetitive cycle of sunspots is near to being fathomed.

There is a "peak and pit" sunspot cycle estimated at eleven years. There is also an approximate forty to forty-five year period within which there's an increase of sun storms (solar flares). Mounting evidence suggests that an increase in sunspots and solar flares seems to induce a trend towards warm-dry conditions here on earth. Likewise, declining solar activity is marked by the onset of a planetary shift to cold-wet conditions.

The change in the weather caused by varying solar action has a direct influence on the behavior of humans. Research indicates that warm periods are marked by dictators, despotism, and global wars. Warm was the cycle during Diocletian's persecutions of the Christians in Rome, and, quoting J. D. Ratcliff: "Ninety percent of the Jewish persecutions occurred in warm periods." (*Nation's Business*)

On the other hand, cold eras are characterized by democracy, social reforms, and civil wars. Joseph Goodavage, author of *Storm on the Sun* states that "Ninety-two percent of the kings and leaders whom history proclaimed as 'great' lived during cold periods." Such cold era "greats" include:

Jesus	Luther	Martin Luther King
Constantine	Calvin	Billy Graham

Though the cyclic pattern of sunspots has been charted and graphed for over four decades, it is still yet to be discovered why the periodic waxing and waning occurs. In his book *Death of the Sun,* John Gribbin substitutes the words "sunspots and solar flares" with the powerful phraseology *Fatal Flickers*. Are sunspots an indication that ole' Sol is just about to burn out?

Scientists confidently state that the sun *will* die in another 4,000-5,000 million years. How they arrived at that particular figure I do not know. I do know though that the "recent" idea of sundoom is biblically substantiated. In fact, the gradual demise of the sun is inferred throughout The Revelation. Symptoms of eventual solar extermination are dealt with when the Sixth Seal is opened, when the Fourth Trumpet is blown, and when the Fourth Bowl is spilt.

THE SIXTH SEAL — Revelation 6:12. "I watched as he broke the sixth seal, and there was a vast earthquake and the sun became dark like black cloth, and the moon was blood-red."

Close comparisons between geological records and sun cycle data have led scientists to conclude that the amount of convulsive action here on earth is directly proportional to the amount of solar activity during solar storms, in process immediately before the earth-action. The "bursts" of energy released by the sun cause the undue stresses on volcanoes and fault lines, hence dormant mounts come alive, and steady ground begins to tremble.

The sun will not be extinquished by the breaking of the Sixth Seal. The sun is mentioned numerous times after the sixth seal breakage. However, the sun will become "dark like black cloth" as it is shrouded by the thick ash-cloud thrust aloft by the coughing mountains around the world. It is also the volcanic ash that will give the moon a "blood red" appearance. (see chapter 21)

THE FOURTH TRUMPET — Revelation 8:12. "The fourth angel blew his trumpet and immediately a third of the sun was blighted and darkened, and a third of the moon and the stars, so that the daylight was dimmed by a third, and the nighttime darkness deepened."

What could "blight" and darken one-third of the sun? — Sunspots. Our sun is figured to be one million miles in diameter; individual spots range from 800-8,000 miles across. During peak periods of spottiness, professional observers count hundreds of sun blotches daily. Therefore, we must realize that some minor fraction of the sun is already blighted and darkened. If there should be a drastic increase in the quantity of spots, or if one single sunspot were to rapidly grow to massive proportions, the segment of the sun "blighted" would become much greater and noticeable even to people who seldom glance skyward.

THE FOURTH BOWL — Revelation 16:8. "Then the fourth angel poured out his flask upon the sun, causing it to scorch all men with its fire."

If I were to put this same Scripture in my own words, it would read something like this: "Next the fourth angel caused an incredible solar flare; a flare that destroyed the ozone and allowed strong ultraviolet radiation to reach the skin of humankind."

If you assume, as I do, that the sun darkening (Fourth Trumpet) is caused by sunspots, then the flare-up described in the Fourth Bowl comes as no surprise. Sunspots are the premonition that the solar flares are imminent. The flares (explosions) usually originate from the outer edges of sunspots and send bursts of solar energy upward. These concentrated energy emissions are quite capable of altering the composition of our atmosphere, (in August 1972 the biggest flare yet to be recorded temporarily produced a 10% decrease in the ozone layer.) thereby making earth-life intolerable and/or impossible. According to John Gribbon, author of *The Death of the Sun:* "A great solar flare at the right (or wrong!) time could all but remove the ozone layer which protects us from ultraviolet radiation, with the result that the land surface could be almost sterilized, with large plants and animals being wiped out, before the natural chemical balance is restored."

To human beings, the consequence of exposure to excessive ultraviolet radiation could mean widespread skin cancer, characterized by "pains and sores." (see Revelation 16:10, 11) The National Academy of Science estimates that just a 5% decrease in ozone could lead to at least 8,000 additional cases of skin cancer annually in the United States. Considering the current number of reported skin cancer victims (300,000-600,000 per year), a total depletion of the ozone could result in a minimum of 160,000 new skin cancer sufferers in just this country. The global figures would reach staggering levels . . . "and his subjects gnawed their tongues in anguish, and cursed the God of heaven for their pains and sores." (Revelation 16:10b, 11)

The freakish demeanor of the sun in the Revelation is undeniably fearsome. However, there is a happy ending to the story. When the sun is completely obliterated, it will NOT be missed. God himself will provide the light by his presence.

> *"In that city which Christ has prepared for His own there will be no created light, simply because Christ Himself, who is the uncreated light (John 8:12), will be there . . . The created lights of God and of men are as darkness when compared with our Blessed Lord. The light He defuses throughout eternity is the unclouded, undimmed glory of His own Holy Presence. In consequence of the fullness of that light, there shall be no night."*
>
> Dr. Lehman Strauss

Sun Fun

"Above the rest, the sun who never lies,
Foretells the change of weather in the skies;
For if he rise unwilling to his race
Clouds on his brow and spots upon his face,
Or if through mists he shoots his sullen beams,
Frugal of light in loose and straggling streams,
Suspect a drizzling day and southern rain,
Fatal to fruits and flocks, and promised grain."

— Virgil

"The sun reveals the secrets of the sky,
And who dares give the source of light the lie.

The sunflower was worshiped by the Inca Indians as an earthly symbol of their supreme deity, a sun-god. Today the sunflower is used in soapmaking, candle making, lighting, cosmetics, bird and cattle feed, poultry mixture, human snack food, and even a few home "cure-all" concoctions.

Sun in one's eyes (To have the) . . . to be tipsy
Brewer's *Dictionary of Phrase and Fable*

SUNDAY SAINT: A faithful church-goer who is strictly religious on Sunday, but is noticeably "loose" the remaining six days of the week.

St. Petersburg, Florida *gives away* newspapers on days the sun doesn't shine.

How to use your watch as a compass . . . Sight down the hour hand toward the sun. The imaginary line from 12 through 6 will point to north.

"In the days of sunshine, so live that in the days of rain you will still be happy."

Twinkle, Twinkle, out there far
Sun, you are a super star.
Tanning bronze my pale bod —
Product of the Lord my God *

Shake and Quake

Rattle, rumble
Shimmer, shake
Flaming mountains
Tremor, quake
On the increase,
Many fear
All this means
The End is near *

"It feels to me like earthquake weather" is a time-worn expression now seldom heard beyond the premises of an old hermit's homestead. There was a time though, when the "signs" were taught and precautions taken. The earthquake weather concept was based on the assumption that hot and dry, stagnated weather encourages earthquake activity. Sure, it may sound ludicrous, but the earthquake weather idea was fostered by a very basic, back-yard observation: When moisture is unavailable, miniscule fault lines begin to crack erratic paths across the sun-parched ground. Due to the fact that meterological proof in support of earthquake weather was non-existent, the notion was cast into posterity's "pit" pot of old wives' tales.

It is now generally believed that neither volcanoes nor earthquakes are resultant of particular types of weather; however both are quite capable of altering existing weather and at times can create their own atmospheric phenomena. Of utmost importance is that studies definitely reveal that short-term weather and long-term climate have both been affected by volcanic and/or seismic activity, on local and global levels. It is projected that these great geological disturbances will largely account for the freakish weather patterns prophesied prior to the close of the age.

Fires are the biggest weather-changing threat spawned by earthquakes. Sparked by live wires and fractured fuel tanks, raging fires are capable of feeding thick smoke columns into the air for days after a quake, causing the formation of a smoke-screen in the upper levels of the atmosphere, upsetting the normal heat balance.

Likewise, volcanic ash hurled high into the stratosphere can create worldwide temperature anomalies. According to William Humphrey (first documenter of weather-volcano relations): Volcanic dust is some thirty times more effective in keeping the sun's radiation out than trapping the earth's radiation *in*. Therefore, a gradual planetary cooling is imminent following a major eruption. In fact, it is theorized that subsequent emissions of volcanic dust, added to the stratosphere as often as every two years, "would continuously maintain a temperature low enough to cover the earth with a mantle of snow so extensive as to be self-perpetuating, and thereby initiate at least a cool period, or under the most favorable conditions, even an ice age." (William Humphrey, *American Weather Stories*, p. 48)

A most interesting find along this line involves the extreme subterranean volcanic activity that is biblically recounted as having occurred in conjunction with the forty-day Noachic Deluge. (see Chapter 6) Prior to flood-time, it is assumed that the earth was universally temperate. To verify this warm-weather concept, archaelogists have unearthed and presented tropical plant and animal fossils from locations representative of all existing climates, including both polar regions. Creationists and evolutionists though in disagreement on the timing by some 90,000 years do share the same theory that it was volcanic dust, suspended aloft following a calamitous event, that caused the rapid cooling which glaciated the poles, and eradicated many species of antidiluvian fauna and flora. To quote Nigel Calder, author of *Weather Machine*, "Casting around for possible explanations for the sudden cooling of 90,000 years ago the scientists see only two obvious mechanisms that might be capable of acting with sufficient speed. One would be enormous volcanic eruption or sequence of eruptions."

Occasionally a major volcanic expulsion will emit such huge quantities of debris into the sky that the newly created ash cloud is thick enough to effectively "black out" the sun. This condition has been repeatedly demonstrated over the years, with persons located downwind of eruptions anxiously relating how a "mysterious darkness" slowly but silently consumed the sun. Following the simultaneous eruption of three mountains of the Alaskan range during July 1953, headlines in the *Anchorage Daily News* (July 9) announced "City Blacked Out by Three Volcanoes," with details reporting an uncanny "blackout over 10,000 square miles of western Alaska." Strangely enough though, some nearby towns were seemingly spared from darkness and enjoyed a clear sunny day, while others lived with gloom.

In the early 1960s, an Italian archaeologist, Angelos Galanopoulos, formally presented a systematic theory correlating non-elliptical, mid-day blackouts and volcanic eruptions. In particular Galanopoulos revived an earlier released supposition associating the biblical "plague of darkness" (Exodus 10:22) with the timely eruption of Mt. Thera. Moses, forewarned by God, pointed to the sky and commanded darkness to come just as the leading edge of Thera's ash-cloud began obscuring the sky. Due to the steering winds, the ash-cloud remained confined in its drift to the airspace over the Egyptian territory, and the sky above the land inhabited by the Chosen People was filled with sunshine as usual.

Galanopoulos' supposition, though impossible to verify, seems logical. Noting the characteristics of more recently formed ash-clouds, it has been observed that each thick, narrow cloud has well-defined side boundaries, thus accounting for the abrupt changeover from dark to light. Depending almost entirely on the prevailing winds after the volcanic eruption, some communities are left to observe clear skies, whereas residents in neighboring towns are faced with premature darkness.

Besides distorting one's view of the sun, high concentrations of volcanic dust in the atmosphere can also influence the appearance of the moon. Like all particulants suspended aloft, volcanic dust filters the moonlight and gives the moon an unexpected hue. If the volcanic dust is moisture laden, then the moon's face is blushed "blood red" (Revelation 6:12). On the other hand, the presence of dry volcanic dust gives the moon a blue visage. The blue coloring occurs very seldom. So seldom, in fact, that the expression, "once in a blue moon" has come to mean "a rare event," like two full moons in one calendar month (The first time this reference was made was December 10, 1883, following the eruption of Krakotoa.)

"Smash" (a combination of smoke and ash), "black blizzard," and "gray rain" are three terms used exclusively in describing bizarre weather outcomes of volcanism. Falling from the sky like unchilled, dirty snow, volcanic ash can accumulate in shovelable drifts in areas downwind from an eruption, causing hazardous driving conditions, aircraft delays, and breathing difficulties. Within close range, even more serious side-effects are imminent. Molten materials and poisonous gases can burn, choke, cripple and/or kill any form of life in the vicinity of a "live" mountain. According to *Newsweek* (June 2, 1980) the after-scene resembles "pictures you see on late night TV of the world blowing up," with eye witnesses speaking "in terms of biblical wrath or nuclear Armageddon."

A common, brief description of the awful, sudden downpour of hot grit and gases is "it rained *fire and brimstone.*" This expression is a near-direct extraction from Psalms 11:6, "He will rain down fire and brimstone on the wicked . . ." Never knowing just exactly what "brimstone" was, I thumbed through my desk dictionary and came across a simple definition; "sulphur." How coincidental it then seemed to me that the toxic fumes emitted from Mount St. Helens were also determined to be "sulphurous." Could it be that a fallout of fire and brimstone will be supplied by many erupting volcanoes during the Judgment Period?

Actually, volcanoes are not even cited in the End-time prophecies. However, their geological counterpart, earthquakes, are specified as being active agents signaling the Second Coming. And, because of mounting evidence interrelating these two forces, it has thereby been deduced that increased volcanism will also play a major role in Apocalyptic events. It is this reasoning that caused the instantaneous "awareness of the hour" when the dormant St. Helens reawakened.

Mount St. Helens, more so than any other volcano in

memorable history, is being deemed a prime portent by contemporary doom-sayers. Though the mountain has erupted numerous times in its lifetime (carbon-dated at 37,000 years), its recent restlessness is especially alarming since it comes at a time when many other prophecies are being fulfilled. Its proximity to a coastline (among other things) has led some to speculate that it is the "great mountain burning with fire" to be cast into the sea following the Second Trumpet Blast. (Revelation 8:8 KJV) Additional attention is awarded Mount St. Helens simply because of its "religious" name. Previously known as Fire Mountain by the resident Cowlitz Indians, George Vancouver retitled the peak St. Helens in honor of England's ambassador to Spain, St. Helens. The religious symbolism, though, far pre-dates the English emissary and explorer. Saint Helen, the mother of Constantine (A.D. 274) is accredited with the discovery of Our Saviour's Cross. Nearly three centuries after the crucifixion, during a lull in Christian zeal, Helen rekindled the dying flame of Christianity because of her magnificent "Find." Today, religious analysts suspect the eruption of Mount St. Helens will lead to a similar religious revelation and trigger a mass conversion to Christianity worldwide.

Whether or not St. Helens, singularly, is salient in the End-time happenings is purely speculative. However, concrete and factual are the statistics assembled by the Solar Terrestrial Data Center in Boulder, Colorado, that indicate earth tremors, of all proportions, are on a decisive increase. The most significant augmentation has been in vibrations registering over 6.5 on the Richter scale. (The Richter scale is logarithmic. Each ONE point increase is indicative of an earthquake TEN times larger than the former number. The San Francisco quake of 1906 measured 11.) This trend, which seismologists project *will* continue, coincides neatly with a major sign of the parousia, "great earthquakes occurring in many lands." (Matthew 24:7, Mark 13:8 and Luke 21:11)

The recently accepted theory, known as *global plate tectonics*, (First developed in the early 1900s by Alfred Wegener) partially explains why earthquakes occur where they do. Scientists supporting this theory believe the earth's crust is subdivided into many *plates* which resemble parts of a loosely-assembled jigsaw puzzle. The places where the plates come close together, as if to interconnect, are known as *faults*. At all times, the plates are in silent, subtle motion but occasionally the movement is swift and violent, hence earthquakes and related geological convulsions like volcanoes.

The plate tectonics theory does account for why earthquakes occur, but no provision in the sophisticated theory satisfactorily explains the crescendo in earthquake activity during the last two decades. Normal seismic activity is "guestimated" to be not in excess of a few inches, annually. However, an earthquake can accomplish more than a century's worth of movement in less than a minute, creating large fissures two and three feet across.

A number of earthquake cause-effect explanations have been offered by geologists, seismologists, and "ologists" of other scientific persuasion. Many of the more recent assumptions parallel the feelings of Dr. Jeffrey Goodman; "Man himself is cocking the hammer for the earth's next cataclysmic blast." (*Globe:* August 26, 1980). In an effort to make this planet more hospitable, humankind has gorged, bombed, and burrowed into the earth's "body," redistributing many of the natural stress points. The long-term consequences are now being experienced.

If the global plate tectonics hypothesis is correct, then we are living on sixty-mile thick "rafts" floating on a liquid "ocean" of molten matter. Each time we drill a well, carve a tunnel, blast a bomb, we are "rocking the boat," causing a series of minor ripples that cause other rafts, adrift nearby, to also wobble and possibly bump into each other.

In 1978, an earthquake in Iran claimed the lives of over 25,000 persons. The earthquake is believed to have been triggered by a ten megaton underground nuclear test, set off by the Soviet Union just thirty-six hours before the disastrous quake. Similar calamitous events are also now being linked to humankind's fascination and frolic with mutilating Mother Earth. It does appear truthful that we are, as Dr. Goodman stated, "cocking the hammer." If this is the case, we can only expect eventual punishment: Revelation 11:18 (KJV): He will "destroy them which destroy the earth."

The acceleration and magnification of earthquakes, in general, are the preparatory procedures, forerunning the most significant quake yet to strike: the quake that splits the Mount of Olives. This quake, prophesied by Zechariah (Zechariah 14:4) long before modern seismological equipment, will halve the Mount of Olives from east to west, beginning at the moment Christ's foot first retouches the earth. For more than twenty centuries, this prediction was accepted but not substantiated. However, recently an oil company's investigative group stumbled upon the huge fault while surveying a sight for oil wells east of Jerusalem. The discovered fault line is located exactly as scripturally prescribed (see below) and is thought to be capable of separation at anytime.

Zechariah 14:4 (KJV): "And his feet shall stand in that day upon the Mount of Olives, which is before Jerusalem on the east, and the Mount of Olives shall cleave in the midst thereof toward the east and toward the west, and there shall be a very great valley; and half of the mountain shall remove toward the north, and half of it toward the south."

Everybody's got the shakes
(Ants in pants, galore)
Rock and roll is here to stay
(Twist and shout some more),

Heebie-jeebies, jitterbug,
Quakey? Shakey? Move!
"Upsee-Dutch" and "Topsy-Turve"
(Alas, you're in the "groove"!)
Keep it up but, man, "get-down,"
Everybody "swings."
So much motion, Will we know,
*Just WHO the Big Quake brings?**

Holy Hyetological* Hoaxes!

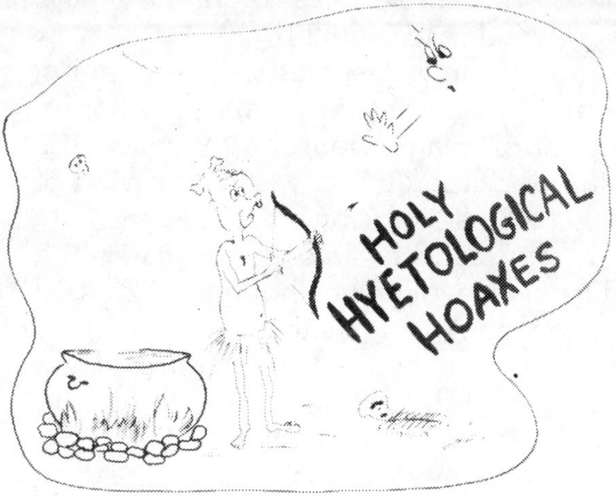

Thanks to *Maverick*, *Gunsmoke*, *Cheyenne*, *Bonanza*, and several other hit TV westerns of the late 50s and 60s, my mind's eye sees drought as a dusty, dry-throated cowboy desperately struggling to stumble across a desolate desert. However, in reality, drought is much worse than withered cactus plants and dehydrated rattlesnakes. Drought is deadly.

For years, weather handbooks have treated drought as a meteorological anomaly, discussing it as an unusual event that rarely occurs. This old-fashioned idea has recently been proven false, though, as new methods of tracing past droughts have been developed. In particular, tree-ring research has provided a wealth of evidence indicating that drought is a recurrent condition which burdens one area or another, year after year. From all corners of the world, pencil-thin columns of wood have been extracted from ancient trees, and the annual growth

*Hyetology — study of rain, snow, etc.

rings have been closely examined. Thin rings are representative of years with minimal water supply and all but a few of the sample trees cored and analyzed reveal stunted growth due to drought.

Because of the widespread and frequent occurrence of drought, through the ages humankind has expended a vast amount of imagination and invention on resisting, preventing or ceasing the devastating period of dryness. Presently, professional cloud seeders are hired to emit chemical "rain-inducers" into clouds via aircraft. Prior to the Industrial Revolution, though, a number of less sophisticated rainmaking methods were attempted.

Prayer was the primary procedure of encouraging clouds to relinquish their rain. Aware of *who* guarded and governed the weather, folks petitioned the Man in Charge for much-needed rain. Fearing the drought was a consequence of their sin, townspeople banded together to beg for divine mercy, promising to amend and improve their disgraceful life styles.

This type of supplication was scripturally founded on the words of Moses from Deuteronomy 28:1a, 12a: "If you fully obey all these commandments of the Lord your God, . . . He will open to you his wonderful treasury of rain in the heavens, to give you fine crops every season."

Another not-so-subtle technique used to coax clouds to release rain was based on religious revenge. If desired wet weather did not come to pass, valued statues of favored saints were severely maltreated. A few of the fine figures were extirpated and stood on their heads. Others were dishonored by having black shrouds placed over their faces. A few statues were permanently banished from drought-struck areas, and one patron saint was even robbed of his wings!!

During the Middle Ages, the Christian cross was considered a powerful periapt for promoting precipitation. Farmers, concerned about their planted fields, erected large crosses in their planted fields to protect crops from adverse weather conditions and to insure a hearty harvest. The crosses were intended to be visible markers for the Lord to see where his help was required the most.

A more popular religious device that heydayed in times of drought was the divining rod. As the name implies, the divining rod was initially believed to be divine; an adjective Webster defines as "given or inspired by God." Listed as a synonym to divining rod is *Aaron's Rod.* Herein lies the biblical connection to the utensil now deemed to be as silly and senseless as a store-bought Ouija Board:

> *Aaron was the brother of Moses. As is recounted in Numbers 20, the Israelites were more than ill-humored by the Exodus incident that eventually led them into a no-man's land void of food and water. Feeling quilty, Moses and Aaron, the leaders of the group, requested assistance from the Lord. In response to their request, God instructed Moses to take the rod of Aaron and command a rock to give forth water. Acting as advised, Moses "drew" water from "nowhere," with the aid of Aaron's "divine" rod.*

In attempts to reiterate this biblical miracle, the divining rod came into being. Each rod was carefully selected and operated according to specified requirements inferred by Scripture. e.g. the rods were forked branches of an almond tree. (Numbers 17:8, . . . Aaron's rod had blossomed and yielded nuts.) The rod had to be held with palms facing up (a position denoting a desire to show mercy) (Proverbs 1:24 and Isaiah 65:2)

Archaeologists are uncertain as to exactly when the first diving rods were employed; however, facsimilies of the water wand have been unearthed and postdated to the time of ancient civilizations of Scythia, Persia, and Media. Here in the United States, dowsers were introduced in the first half of the eighteenth century by English and German settlers who demonstrated the ritual to interested colonists. Not long thereafter, though, the rods began to be denounced as implements of heresy, and persons insistent on using divining rods were tagged *water witches*.

Despite excessive public harassment, the art of dowsing continued to be practiced and even in today's society, amidst test-tube baby experiments and heart transplant victims, there are 25,000 persons in this country that profess to be water witches. Unfortunately, the majority of contemporary water witches are ignorant of the rod's holy heritage, and instead are members of the ever-enlarging clan of cult con men. Associates of astrologers and pals of palm readers, modern water witches vie on voodooism to receive good vibes, summoning Satan to steer them to hidden water sources. Once the evil spirits have been contacted, the rod begins to twitch and tremor, until finally it makes a sudden dip downward to a plot of innocent dry land. Under this spot lies the expected underground water source.

True, this irreligious procedure is far removed from the original event that prompted widespread use of the divining rod, but, nevertheless, each year when water becomes scarce due to lack of rainfall, water witches are sought and paid phenomenal fees to help solve the drought problems.

H_2O
Where did you go?
It hasn't rained for days.

My lawn is dead,
My skin is red,
No clouds above; just haze.

What can we do?
Who can we sue?
and will it all get worse?

Like hell, it's hot,
It's called a drought,
. . . and is the devil's curse. *

Sow What?

The sun's been out for days on end
My skin is burnt past tan,
My lawn is parched, my garden dry,
And there's a water ban.

Of course, I said, "I hate dark skies,"
"Rain, rain; please go away!"
(I can't have picnics if it's wet,
And baseball I can't play.)

But now I'd sell my soul for rain,
Without it we'll all die;
"$2.98," the Devil said.
Sure, go ahead and try.

So, with some chemicals in hand
(Like fairy-tale dust),
The clouds are drugged and coaxed to crack.
. . . God looks down with disgust. *

. . . "For they have sown the wind, and they shall reap the whirlwind."

With the numerous scripts currently available on the topic of weather modification, it would be difficult to place correct authorship on the above quote. This particular quote, though, is not to be forgotten. The penman: Hosea; the reference: The Holy Bible. (Hosea 8:7 KJV)

Amazing? Yes. The end-time prophecy takes into account people meddling with meteorological matters, even though such operations were totally unheard of at the time of the prediction, nearly 800 years before the birth of Christ.

Unfortunately, this key verse of Scripture has gotten lost in the hoard of other biblical "just waits" that scientists disregard and evangelists overlook. Instead, through scant, one-sided articles produced by mass media sources, society has been brainwashed into thinking that climate control is our future salvation, a way to tame storms, quench drought-thirsty grounds, and warm winters. We've been led to believe that life would be no less than grandiose in the Camelot climate designed and directed by humans. To everyone's advantage, prosperity would abound.

But, how much will it cost us to achieve this idealistic set-up? How much has it cost already? Turning over the price tag a bit later, let's first consider payment through human lives. Have we already self-induced tragedies by permitting atmospheric alterations by fellow humans?

Records reveal that numerous cloud seeding endeavors have been *overly* successful. For instance, in January 1916, famed rainmaker Charles Warren Hatfield, was contracted by the San Diego city council to "create" rain in that drought-struck town. It was agreed that Hatfield would be paid $1,000 *per inch* of artificially induced precipitation. A funny thing happened, though; instead of the desired "moderate, beneficial rainfall," an incredible *twenty inches* of driving rains flooded the area, killed seventeen people, and demolished the nearby Lower Otay Dam! Hatfield was lucky to escape town with his life, never attempting to collect his promised "reward."

More recently, a record flood ravaged Rapid City, South Dakota, (June 1972) only several hours after a government plane seeded the skies nearby. Two hundred persons drowned in the floodwaters, with property losses mounting into the millions. The surviving residents who were aware of the federal finagling were furious and were quick to place the blame on the near-to-obvious culprit, the rainmaker. Eventually, the charges filed against the government were dropped. The reason? There was no way of proving *beyond a reasonable doubt,* what the natural weather would have done if the cloud seeders hadn't interfered.

And so it goes; nothing can be proved or disproved when it comes to weather modification, but extensive research continues with our atmosphere at risk, tenuously teased, tested, and tortured like some destined-to-die laboratory rat. Model mathematical equations are assembled and assessed, never to be solved because each quantity is a variable.

No one knows what *can* happen, *does* happen or *will* happen as a result of weather modification endeavors. Regardless of these facts, though, government agencies are quick to take credit for sponsoring seemingly successful results, but, on the other hand, deny even partial responsibility for life-claiming calamities. A federal fiasco . . . a federal fiasco financed by *our* tax dollars.

Supposedly, it is because of possible public resistance and widespread alarmism that the American populace is intentionally kept vaguely informed about weather modification projects. Probably for the same reasons, the huge sums of money allocated for such projects are also kept "hush-hush," cleverly camouflaged in the "other" or "miscellaneous" category. Such plans, though, consume a selfish slice of the budget pie, with twenty million dollars spent annually (as of 1980) to seed clouds, suppress hail and disperse fogs.

This silent drain of federal moneys began over ninety years ago! In 1890, the United States Congress appropriated $19,000 for weather modification activities to be administered by the U.S. Department of Agriculture. The projects were to include ventures into the experimentations that earlier had led Ruggles and Atwater to patents for rainmaking and tornado dissipation in the years 1880 and 1887, respectively.

Conducting the government's first funded weather modification experiments was a man named General Robert St. George Dyrenforth. Indications are that Dyrenforth earned a substantial number of believers as a result of his work, since, as expected, the government was quick and complete in glamourously reporting one cloud cannonading that coincided with a downpour of significant proportions. No mention is made, though, of Dyrenforth's other four attempts, so we can safely assume they were failures.

Weather modification continued to be supported by the government for some forty to fifty years, with the cloud-seeding business booming to prosperity, reaching its peak in the early 1950's. At that time, the skies spanning nearly 10% of the continental United States were seeded. By 1965, though, the percentages of seeded skies had been drastically reduced to 3%, and today (we are told) cloud seeding operations are limited to only 1.3% of the country's acreage. Why?

The marked decrease in reported cloud seeding events has nearly paralleled the marked increase in legal problems regarding humans' meteorological manipulation. Lawsuits against "seeders" have confronted judges with unique and truly uncanny charges, like *premediated flooding* and *rain theft.* Climatological court cases have emerged which involve a threat against our foremost constitutional assurance; the right to certain unalienable rights, like life, liberty and the pursuit of happiness.

The exact legal problem seems to specifically involve the pursuer and pursuee. Is it rightful to seed clouds to produce the ideal rainfall for *our* crops, when the same amount of rain would ruin the products of a nearby neighbor? Should a hurricane be "killed" in order to prevent flood damage in one area, even though the storm's death would create a deadly drought in another area?

When questions like these are considered, the magnificence of our meteorological manipulation is sharply reduced. The varied elements of weather act and react like balanced bowling pins; when one pin is agitated, all others are affected. Who's right when we're all wrong?

But, this growing problem of legality in weather matters in not new. It dates back into the early 1700s. At that time, the practice of hailstorm shooting was widespread. Guns were fired into high-topped thunder clouds in attempts to "blow apart" large chunks of destructive hail. The mortar was often ignited with the ends of candles that had been burned at Candlemas ceremonies (see Chapter 7) and specially blessed to save farmers from a possible hail "bombing." As often as not, though, ruinous hail fell anyway. If it happened that hail blasted the lands of an anti-hail suppression advocate, blame was instantly placed on the hail shooters. Disputes arose.

In 1750, the Archduchess, Maria Theresa of Austria, officially recognized the problem and eliminated the grounds of discontent by issuing a royal decree outlawing the skyward shooting of guns. For similar reasons, in the late 1700s, the British Empire banned the ringing of church bells during storms. The popularity of bell ringing, though, was overwhelming, and to this day, church bells continue to ring loudly in many European countries in belief it will prevent lightning and windstorms (see Chapter 14).

In the United States, the first lawsuit involving cloud seeding was formally filed in 1950:

SLUTSKY et. al. versus the STATE OF NEW YORK. Slutsky, a resort owner in Ulster County, New York, filed suit against New York because the state had engaged the services of a noted rainmaker as a solution to end a horrid drought. Slutsky claimed the seeding, if successful, would infringe on his business, since vacationers stay at home when rain falls. Below is the court's final decision:

> "The court must balance the conflicting interests between a remote possibility of inconvenience to plaintiffs and its guests with the problem of maintaining and supplying the inhabitants of the city of New York and surrounding areas, with a population of about 10 million inhabitants, with an adequate supply of pure and wholesome water. The relief which the plaintiffs ask is opposed to the general welfare and public good; and the dangers which plaintiffs apprehend are purely speculative. This court will not protect a possible injury at the expense of public advantage."[1]

The decision on this particular case seemed cut and dried and was not appealed. Since the early 1950s, though, scores of less simple cases have been filed and argued extensively. So it seems quite obvious and logical that one reason we should *not* interfere with natural weather occurrences is because, inevitably, it breeds

---

1. D. S. Halacy, Jr. *The Weather Changers*, (Harper and Row, 1968), p. 214.

contempt. Contempt eventually leads to conflict, and conflict among local residents can result in rioting. Riots, in turn, are forerunners of civil war situations, and, in this day and age, our country certainly needs no internal problems to further weaken our stand internationally. Just imagine the consequences *if* the lawsuit contemplated in 1977 had actually gone to court: Idaho vs. Washington: One state suing another on the account of "supposed" *rain theft*. (Luckily, charges were dropped.)

What is the national government doing to prevent and/or avoid interstate weather rivalries? Virtually nothing. There is no central agency coordinating and overseeing the numerous weather alteration projects now being conducted. Granted, thirty-three states do have laws governing acts of intentional weather tampering. However, since the weather is no respecter of invisible boundaries, it blindly stumbles across geographical state borderlines, interfering and infringing on the lawful rights of a neighboring state whose regulations undoubtedly differ from those where the "corrupted" weather originated. To avoid legal hassles and multi-state opposition, weather modification rules need to be agreed upon by the entire populace, in a national election situation. Is it not written "a house divided against itself cannot stand"? (Mark 3:25, and Luke 11:17)

On a larger scale, weather modification has been used mainly as a method of warfare, deliberately tinkering with natural weather processes in order to inflict hardship on an enemy. The United States is actively involved in researching this type of strategy. Weather modification researcher for the U.S. Navy, Dr. Pierre St. Amand, states: "Primarily the work is aimed at giving the U.S. Navy and other armed forces, if they should care to use it, the capability of modifying the environment to their own advantage or disadvantage of an enemy. We regard weather as a weapon. Anything one can use to get his way is a weapon, and the weather is as good as any."

Climatic warfare played an important part during the Vietnam conflict. Over a seven-year period, the U.S. government expended $22 million on cloud seeding operations over Southeast Asia in an effort to inundate the Ho Chi Minh Trail, turning it into a impassible sea of mud, thereby preventing the flow of supplies along the route into the Viet Cong troops.

And, in the ongoing cold war, accumulated data appears very conclusive regarding the suspicion that Russia caused the recent series of wicked winters in the United States. Using theories introduced to electronics by Nikola Telsa in the early 1900s, the earth's magnetic field was altered by strong low frequency radio transmissions emanating from the Soviet Union. Since our upper level winds tend to track with the magnetic field, these energy surpluses effectively created abnormal variances in the airflow over the U.S., resulting in record extremes that baffled climatologists and caused much human suffering.

Not until after the U.S. had experienced its three all-time coldest winters did scientists begin to link the "freakish weather" with Soviet weather modification experiments. During the investigations, similar coincidental calamities were also matched with the electromagnetism escapades of the Soviet Union: e.g. 1) the Great New York City blackout of July 1977; 2) the earthquake in Tangshan, China killing 650,000-800,000 persons on July 23, 1976; and 3) first snows ever recorded in the Bahamas.

All these diversified examples fail to even begin to outline the natural disasters possible of being inflicted on far-off foes through controlled climate change. Mischievous meteorological acts could be plotted and performed by any government (or group) financially and intellectually capable of supporting the functions. Casuality lists could become longer than those of a full-scale war, with entire civilizations slowly disappearing, frozen, flooded or starved by angry avengers.

The "advantage" to weather warfare is best summed up in the following statement by Dr. Gordon McDonald, of Dartmouth College: "Such a secret war never need be declared nor ever known by the affected population. It could go on for years with only the security forces involved being aware of it. The years of drought and storm could be attributed to unkindly nature, and only after a nation was drained would armed takeover be attempted." (1974 Senate Foreign Relations Committee)

Regardless of intended use, weather modification is much more of a wager than a science. We spend money to play the game, never certain of knowing if we'll walk away with the jackpot or shy home "flat busted." *Reader's Digest* (May 1980, p. 116) states: "Modern cloud seeders generally agree they cannot guarantee what any single cloud will do when they seed it." Likewise, *Discover* (October 1980, p. 24) lists several interesting comments concerning hurricane hampering, "Project Stormfury:" . . . "it may be one of the most daring assaults on nature ever attempted" and "There is some concern that "Stormfury" could backfire."

Why do we continue to *gamble*? How long will it be before the "gospel truth" is realized:

"They have sown the wind, and they shall reap the whirlwind."

Sowing in the morning, sowing seeds of "kindness"
We can make it rain on parched and thirsty ground.
Waiting for the harvest, and the time of reaping . . .
Silver iodide we've tossed in every cloud.

Bringing in the sheaves? We're a bunch of thieves.
Tampering with the weather, tricks stashed up our sleeves.
Like the autumn leaves, fallen from the trees,

*We have left the Father . . . WAIT until the BREEZE**
(to the tune of "Bringing in the Sheaves")

by George A. Minor

Weltuntergangswetter

(German for: Weather for the end of the World)

Partly cloudy, mostly clear,
Gee, this weather's acting queer.
Record highs. All-time lows,
Not a breath, then "thar she blows!"

Feast or famine? Drought or flood?
Dust storms or knee-deep in mud?
Tranquil? Tempest? Ice or fire?
*Just how will this age expire?**

Our weather is changing. One need not be a multi-degreed scientist to make such an astute observation. Normalcy has suddenly become an oddity in daily weather, gradually forcing the term "climate" into obsolescence. Repeatedly, forecasters are humiliated by freak weather changes. Predictions for cool-wet summers (as were so popular after the Mount St. Helens eruption in 1980) have been succeeded by record heat and severe drought. On the other hand, premonitions of intensely cold winters have been followed by summer's warmth. (An excellent illustrative example appeared in the February 19, 1981, *Cleveland Plain Dealer* in an article entitled "Eastern States Roasted:" "The temperature hit 73° at Baltimore, where officials had expected cold weather and closed school for 230,000 pupils for the week to save $100,000 on heating bills.") No one knows what to expect anymore as a variety of weather extremes are proclaimed in news headlines around the world.

Whatever happened to the *ordinary* weather and the *standard* climatic conditions our life styles, industries, and economies have relied upon for so long? Who antagonized mild-mannered Mother Nature and caused her sweet demeanor to quickly turn sour? The answer to these questions is found in the following quote excerpted from the *Report of the Study of Man's Impact on Climate* (SMIC, conducted in 1971, was sponsored by the Massachusetts Institute of Technology.) "There can be little doubt that man, in the process of reshaping his environment in many ways, has changed the climate of large regions of the earth, and he has probably had some influence on global climate as well."

Few scientists will deny the fact that humankind has self-induced many of the weather wounds now panging our planet. In haste to make human living more convenient and carefree, the sensitivities of the earth and its atmosphere have been ruthlessly ignored. Vast expanses of land have been resurfaced with asphalt and cement, and dense forests have been felled to allow the installment of housing projects and businesses. These "improvements" have altered the degree to which the land reflects and absorbs sunlight, hence disrupting the natural planetary heat balance.

Likewise, industry and modern modes of transportation have also interfered, significantly, with the earth's intended heat balance. Since the beginning of the Industrial Revolution, enormous quantities of carbon dioxide have been emitted into the atmosphere, creating a colorless, odorless gas shield that encircles the entire globe. This invisible "lid" prohibits the normal out-flow of heat radiation, and might be causing the earth to steadily warm. Some climatologists believe that this "runaway greenhouse effect" will eventually lead the earth into a catastrophic heat predicament, known as the Venus Situation. The Venus Situation theory is based on the assumption that the inhospitably hot temperatures of Venus (900 °F) are due to pent-up heat trapped close to the Venetian surface by a thick shroud of CO2.

Contrary to the previous two theories, some experts contend that industry and transportation devices are responsible for a slow, but certain, global cooling. Tons of exhaust particles, continuously coughed into the air, could be deflecting away incoming sunlight, thereby shortening regional growing seasons, and encouraging the advance of continental snow cover.

Besides varying temperatures to one extreme or the other, modern humans' machinery and merrymaking have also been accused of altering rain and snowfall percentages by contributing contaminates to the air via chimneys, stacks, tailpipes, etc. Because of this pollution, the moisture in the air surrounding densely populated areas has no problem whatsoever locating "partner-particulants" needed to become condensation nuclei of rain and snow. Consequently, big cities experience more precipitation and visibility obstructions (fog, smog, haze) than rural areas. One study reports the increase results as follows: "10-15% more snow and rain, 16% more thunderstorms and 60% more fog." (From "Who Will Control the Weather?" by Lowell Ponte, *Reader's Digest*, May 1980.)

Furthermore, artificial rainmaking, hail supressing, fog dispersal and similar deliberate modification projects are believed to be linked to our deteriorating climatic conditions. Environmentalists, as well as a surprising number of specialized scientists, insist that the rash of recent weather extremes is a direct result of thirty years' worth of "hush-hush" experiments, purposely conducted to change the world's weather. The "wonder-what-happens-if-we-do-this" pretenses under which these tests were staged are now being sharply criticized and condemned as being detrimental to the weather.

The list goes on. There seems to be no end to the number of theories suggesting that our ultimate doom will be due to some sort of climatic disaster, actuated by our perpetual assault of the environment. But despite the variety of calamities presented, none of the proposed finales is especially appealing or decidedly relevant. Together, the assorted plans do lean towards the mish-mash of meteorological monstrosities prophesied to occur prior to the birth of World Tomorrow: drought (Amos 4:7-8); earthquakes (Matthew 24:7); excessive heat (Revelation 16:8-9); incredible storms (Revelation 16:20); severe winters (Luke 21:11 — Lamsa Bible). (George Lamsa translated the Bible from Aramic, his native language. Originally the Lamsa Bible was called *The New Testament According to the Easter Text.* Luke 21:11 in the Lamsa Bible reads: "And there will be great earthquakes in different places, and famines and plagues; and there will be alarming sights and great signs will appear from heaven; *and the winters will be severe.*"

Should the upset in current global weather conditions be interpreted as an End-time "sign?" Many theologists say "yes." There has been a chain of amazing affairs, occurring in quick succession, that have recently fulfilled large percentage End-time prophecies, including the erratic weather patterns now in progress. Never before, in all of recorded history, has there been a similar upheaval in worldwide weather, and no return to normalcy is anticipated. Could this all be WELTUNTERGANG-SWETTER; weather for the end of the world? (The *New York Times*, Wednesday, July 23, 1980: "While Amerca Bakes, West Germans Tread Water.")

WEATHER-RELIGION CONCORDANCE

(cross-referenced with *The Living Bible*)

ATMOSPHERE
- Genesis 1:6-8
- Psalms 148:4
- Jeremiah 51:16
- Amos 9:6

CLOUDS
- Genesis 9:13-14, 16, 17
- Exodus 13:21, 22, 24
- Exodus 14:19-20
- Exodus 16:10
- Exodus 19:9
- Exodus 19:16
- Exodus 24:15, 16, 18
- Exodus 33:9-10
- Exodus 34:5-6
- Exodus 40:34-38
- Leviticus 16:2
- Numbers 9:15-18, 20-22
- Numbers 10:11, 12, 34
- Numbers 11:25
- Numbers 12:5, 7, 8
- Numbers 14:14
- Numbers 16:42
- Deuteronomy 1:33
- Deuteronomy 4:11
- Deuteronomy 5:22
- Deuteronomy 31:15
- Judges 20:39
- 2 Samuel 22:10
- 2 Samuel 22:12
- 2 Samuel 23:4
- 1 Kings 8:10
- 1 Kings 18:41, 44, 45
- 2 Chronicles 5:14
- Nehemiah 9:12, 19
- Job 3:5
- Job 7:9
- Job 11:17
- Job 14:2
- Job 22:14
- Job 26:8, 9
- Job 30:15
- Job 36:29
- Job 37:15, 16, 21
- Job 38:9, 35, 37
- Psalm 18:11, 12
- Psalm 29:3
- Psalm 36:5
- Psalm 68:4
- Psalm 78:14, 27
- Psalm 97:2
- Psalm 99:7
- Psalm 104:3
- Psalm 105:31, 39
- Psalm 147:8
- Psalm 148:4
- Proverbs 25:14
- Isaiah 19:1
- Isaiah 25:5, 7
- Isaiah 60:8
- Ecclesiastes 5:17
- Ecclesiastes 11:3
- Ecclesiastes 12:2
- Solomon 3:6
- Isaiah 4:5, 6
- Isaiah 5:6
- Isaiah 9:18
- Lamentations 2:1
- Lamentations 3:44
- Ezekiel 1:4, 5
- Ezekiel 8:11
- Ezekiel 10:3, 4
- Ezekiel 30:3
- Ezekiel 31:3, 10, 14
- Ezekiel 38:16
- Daniel 7:13
- Hosea 2:21, 22
- Hosea 6:4
- Nahum 1:3
- Zephaniah 1:15
- Matthew 17:5
- Matthew 24:30

Matthew 24:38, 39
Luke 6:47-49
Luke 17:27
John 8:12
2 Corinthians 11:26
Hebrews 11:7
1 Peter 3:20
1 Peter 4:6
2 Peter 2:5
2 Peter 3:5, 6
Revelation 12:15, 16

FROST
Exodus 16:14
Job 38:29
Psalm 147:16

HAIL
Exodus 9:18, 19, 21-24
Exodus 9:26, 28, 29, 33
Exodus 10:5, 12, 15
Joshua 10:11
Joshua 38:22, 23
Psalm 18:12, 13
Psalm 78:47
Psalm 105:32
Psalm 147:17
Psalm 148:8
Isaiah 28:2, 17
Isaiah 30:30
Ezekiel 13:11, 13
Ezekiel 38:22
Haggai 2:17
Revelation 11:19
Revelation 16:21

HEAT
Genesis 8:22
Deuteronomy 8:15
Job 6:15-18
Job 24:19
Job 37:17
Psalm 19:6
Psalm 147:18
Proverbs 25:13
Isaiah 4:6
Isaiah 25:4, 5
Isaiah 32:2
Joel 1:19
Jonah 4:6, 8
Luke 12:55
Acts 28:3
James 1:10, 11
Revelation 7:16
Revelation 8:7

ICE
Job 6:15-18
Job 38:29, 30
Psalm 147:18

LIGHTNING
Exodus 9:23
Exodus 19:16
Exodus 20:18
2 Samuel 22:15
2 Kings 1:10, 12, 16
Job 28:26
Job 36:30,32
Job 37:3, 11, 12, 15
Job 38:27, 35
Psalm 18:12, 14
Psalm 29:7
Psalm 78:48
Psalm 97:4
Psalm 105:32
Psalm 135:7
Psalm 144:6
Jeremiah 10:13
Jeremiah 51:16
Ezekiel 1:13, 14
Ezekiel 21:15, 28
Zechariah 9:14
Zechariah 10:1
Matthew 24:27
Matthew 28:3
Luke 10:18
Luke 17:24
Revelation 4:5
Revelation 8:5
Revelation 11:19
Revelation 16:18

Psalm 1:13
Psalm 37:34
Ezekiel 34:26

SHOWERS
Job 24:8
Job 37:6
Psalm 65:10
Psalm 72:6
Psalm 147:8
Ezekiel 34:26
Micah 5:7
Zechariah 10:1
Luke 12:54
Hebrews 6:7

SNOW
2 Samuel 23:20
2 Kings 5:27
Job 6:15-18
Job 24:19
Job 37:6
Job 38:22, 23
Psalm 51:7
Psalm 68:14
Psalm 147:16
Psalm 148:8
Proverbs 26:1
Isaiah 1:18
Isaiah 55:10
Jeremiah 18:14
Daniel 7:9
Revelation 1:14

SPRING
Genesis 8:22
Psalm 72:6
Psalm 147:18
Solomon 2:12
Solomon 6:11
Jeremiah 3:3
Jeremiah 5:23, 24
Hosea 6:3
Mark 13:28

SUMMER
Genesis 8:22
Psalm 74:17
Proverbs 6:8
Proverbs 26:1
Isaiah 18:4, 6
Amos 3:15
Zechariah 14:8
Matthew 24:32
Luke 21:30
John 4:35
James 1:10, 11

SUN
Genesis 1:16
Joshua 10:12
Joshua 10:13, 14
Judges 19:14
2 Samuel 23:4
2 Kings 19:26
2 Kings 20:9
Job 30:28
Psalm 32:4
Psalm 105:39
Matthew 5:45
Matthew 6:22
Matthew 4:6
Mark 9:7
Luke 11:34, 35
James 1:10, 11
Revelation 1:16
Revelation 10:1
Revelation 19:17

STORM
Psalm 89:9
Psalm 107:25
Psalm 107:29
Isaiah 4:6
Isaiah 7:2
Isaiah 17:13
Isaiah 24:20
Isaiah 25:4
Isaiah 27:8
Isaiah 28:17
Isaiah 30:30
Isaiah 32:2
Jeremiah 4:13
Jeremiah 10:13

Zechariah 9:14

WEATHER

Psalm 147:18
Psalm 148:8
Proverbs 25:20
Matthew 16:2, 3
Acts 27:9, 14, 15

BIBLIOGRAPHY

Ponte, Lowell. "Who Will Control the Weather?" *Reader's Digest,* May 1980.

Steep, Clayton. "What Is Happening to Our Weather," *The Plain Truth*, April 1980.

Lachman, Charles. "Did Scientist's Tampering Trigger Killer Heatwave and Hurricane?" *Globe*, August 26, 1980.

Ponte, Lowell. "Who Owns the Weather?" *The Cleveland Plain Dealer*, July 22, 1980.

Young, Louise B. *Earth's Aura*. New York: Avon Books, 1977.

Gibbs, Lee W. "What Is the Truth About Groundhogs?" *The Cleveland Plain Dealer*, February 2, 1980.

DeHann, Dennis J. "Keeping a Low Profile," *Our Daily Bread*. Grand Rapids, Michigan: Radio Bible Class, December 1979/January-February 1980.

Oard, Michael J. "The Flood and the Ice Age," *Ministry*, 1980.

Vinocur, John. "While America Bakes, West Germans Tread Water," *The New York Times*, Wednesday, July 23, 1980.

Richards, H. M. S., Jr. *Earthquake*. Nashville: Southern Publishing Association, 1979.

Bingham, Roger. "Explorers of the Earth Within," *Science* — 80, October 1980.

Minnaert, M. *The Nature of Light and Color in the Open Air*. New York: Dover Publications, Inc.

Schwartz, Alvin. *Going Camping*. New York: Macmillan Company, 1969.

Hughes, Patrick. *American Weather Stories*. Washington, D.C.:U.S. Government Printing Office, Stock Number 003-018-00070-9.

Calder, Nigel. *The Weather Machine*. New York: Penguin Press.

Navarra, John G. *Nature Strikes Back*. Natural History Press.

Moore, Patrick. *The Story of Man and the Stars*. New York: W. W. Norton, 1954.

King, C. Henry. *The Background of Astronomy*. New York: George Braziller, Inc., 1958.

Gribbon, John. *The Death of the Sun*. New York: Delacorte Press, 1980.

Cornwall, Judson. *Heaven*. Van Nuys, California: Bible Voice, Inc.

Wescott, Glenway. *A Calendar of Saints for Unbelievers*.

Harper, The Rev. Howard V. *Days and Customs of All Faiths*. Fleet Publishing Company, 1957.

Whitcomb, John C., and Morris, Henry M. *The Genesis Flood*. Presbyterian Reformed Publishing Company, 1961.

Corliss, William R. *Handbook of Unusual Natural Phenomena*. Glen Arm, Maryland: The Sourcebook Project.

Halacy, D. S. *The Weather Changers*. New York: Harper and Row, Inc.

Lee, Albert. *Weather Wisdom*. Dolphin Books, 1976.

Tufty, Barbara. *1001 Questions Answered About Earthquakes, Avalanches, Floods and Other Natural Disasters*. New York: Dover Publications, Inc.

Goodavage, Joseph. *Storm on the Sun*. New York: The New American Library, Inc., 1979.

Sloane, Eric. *Folklore of American Weather*.

Batan, Louis J. *Harvesting the Clouds*.